COWRIES TO CRYPTO

THE HISTORY OF MONEY, CURRENCY AND WEALTH

Words by Jame DiBiasio

Illustrations by Harry Harrison

Produced by OANDA

ACKNOWLEDGEMENTS

Managing Editor
MELINDA EARSDON

Writer
JAME DIBIASIO

Illustrations
HARRY HARRISON

Fact-checker
JACKIE HORNE

Designer
DEREK HANNAH

Production
DAMON BARNETT

Publisher
DAVID HODGE

Publisher's Cataloguing-in-Publication data

Commemorative edition: ISBN 978-1-7342286-1-8
Hardback edition: ISBN 978-1-7342286-0-1

978-1-7342286-0-1

Commemorative Edition. Printed in Singapore

OK, that completes the section on popular music. The next section is on money. So, assuming everyone is listening, let's start!" So called the quizmaster at our local pub challenge one Wednesday night.

"That's Dave's sweet spot," enthused a fellow team member, fighting to be heard over the PA. The underlying message was clear. Dave, you work in finance so we expect you to score big here. Minimum four out of five correct answers expected.

Ten minutes later – having endured five questions on the history of money – I was really only confident of two answers. Another was possibly correct but the others were little more than wild guesses.

In hindsight, I suppose this was the moment the idea for this book first started to form. In trying to satisfy my own curiosity about the history of currency over the following days, I realised there were very limited sources of information available. And just like that, the idea to create a blast through time on the origins of money, from its infancy to today's crypto phenomenon, was born.

So if, like me, you're stumped by questions about the oldest or the most valuable coin in the world, or you're simply interested in the fascinating story of the evolution of money, please read on. Hopefully it will help you – and me – win future pub quizzes to come.

DAVID HODGE
Chief Marketing Officer, OANDA

CONTENTS

01

COWRIES

In the primitive era, there was no market, only hunting and farming

We have begun to work the land, rather than chase and hunt, because cereals and domesticated animals yield more food. The king and the priest conduct the rain rituals; when those who still chase and hunt come to raid our farms, the king's men kill them. But the king and the high priest do not labour with us in the fields. The palace and the temple are down by the river, surrounded by many houses, warehouses and barracks for the king's soldiers.

There is no market. The people would not recognise the word. There is only tribute. The king decrees how much cereal we must give to feed him and the growing number of priests, generals and courtly retinue – dancers, servants and scribes. You can tell who's who by their finery, especially the necklaces of cowry shells worn by the royal family.

When the king wishes to reward someone for their loyalty, he gives them a string of cowries. If the person is from a noble family, the king will first wrap the shells in gold foil. He now considers these a promise, as good as the words he speaks. A nobleman can go to the warehouse and show the scribe his golden cowry, and the scribe will allot him a bucket of cereal. People wonder what makes the king's gift so valuable. Is it the shell, or the lustrous gold, or is it just that it once belonged to the king?

The goldsmith decides to test this. He has no cowries and has received no gift from the king, but he takes an ingot to the warehouse scribe. Is this enough for a bucket of cereal?

This is how we – people – invented money. We had "commodity" or "proto" money long before we had formal markets. Proto-money originated as items such as cowry shells or cacao seeds, as barrels of rice or heads of cattle. These were commodities that took on an additional use in exchange while retaining their original purpose. This ability to serve dual functions made them extra valuable. And then people with no interest in consuming the goods began to accept them simply because of their usefulness in barter.

Kings would not have invented proto-money. Rulers were happy to exercise control over the existing system of tribute. Once commodities began to be used as a means of payment, though, kings took notice. A system of currency was wonderful – so long as they could manipulate it. Now it would be the king who decided when something was "money". Who was going to argue with him?

Money, currency and wealth are bound up with the story of civilisation. But they are not just inventions. They are concepts whose creation and evolution changed the way people think and interact. Money is both a product of civilisation and a driver of it. This book will focus on those periods of innovation that transformed society. A few of these include – spoiler alert – the inventions of coinage and paper money, the rise of Renaissance Italian banking and the founding of the Bank of England. Today, on the cusp of the 2020s, our world is working through a package of innovation in money, currency and finance that is just as revolutionary, and it is the aim of this book to explain what's continuous with the past, what's genuinely radical and how the game may change yet again.

Before there was money, there was exchange, which we lazily call "barter". But our popular notion of barter as a trade between one person with, say, a block of salt and another with, say, a batch of spears – that idea doesn't work. First of all, these items are not denominated in amounts that are easy to trade. How much salt is worth ten spears? But more importantly, the person with the spears might not need salt so much as a new pair of shoes. If there were no markets, how could any form of cooperation or exchange take place?

People must have relied on brokers to grease the wheels of barter. These third parties could help people get what they wanted by using a token of some kind (such as a cowry shell) to serve as a rate of exchange.

Barter was not peer to peer, but a multi-party affair. The customers want salt or spears; the broker operates because he doesn't want either, but he knows other people who might. And he begins to accumulate tokens to make more barter happen. In other words, the broker begins to save and customers to borrow.

Money and the development of human thought go hand in hand. Money is an abstraction. A token always stands for something else. It is a metaphor. Its adoption was probably an unconscious development. The very first brokers lacked the language to express the idea. Gradually, the need for money would spur the creation of tools to put this idea into conscious form.

The earliest forms of writing were tally marks: scratches or notches in bone, wood or stone, which go back more than 40,000 years to southern Africa. This is the first evidence of when people engaged in barter, which implies this was when some people became middlemen. Prostitution is often called the oldest profession, but surely that honour goes to commodity brokers.

Tallies eventually became symbols or memory aids, a form of proto-writing. The first known examples of such pictographs date back to China's Yellow River valley around 6600BCE, followed a thousand years later along the Danube in Europe.

A "true writing" system, however, is one that mirrors a verbal discussion. The first civilisation to use true writing was the Sumerians in modern-day Iraq (or ancient Mesopotamia, as the area was also known). By the fourth millennium BCE, they had invented a system of ideograms combined with tallies, called cuneiform, which they imprinted onto clay tablets. Why? To track payments for commodities.

Money was already becoming a means of payment and a store of value. The Sumerians expanded the definition to include a record of account. Transactions became bound to what was in clay. In doing so, their concept of money helped spur writing and the idea of a contract.

Sumer and the civilisations that followed – Babylonia plus the ancient worlds of Egypt, China and the Indus River valley – developed accounting and payment systems in which precious metals or other forms of proto-money were used to supplement transactions. Metal ingots or bars came to denote the highest denominations, although their use was restricted to bulk deals.

For everyday transactions, ancient Mesopotamia developed standardised weights for barley. A "talent" was about 30kg, or what a person could carry. This was subdivided into smaller units, down to the shekel, which weighed about 8.3g. Therefore, if merchants accepted a system of weights of barley, brokers could use this as money and accumulate enough to help other people buy and sell (for a fee).

Of course, this put such brokers in a position of instant mistrust, which may explain why the Babylonian Hymn to Samas warned against "he who brings about deception for gain, and changes weights."

Or it might be why an Egyptian instruction manual from around 1200BCE warns would-be tax assessors not "to move the scales nor alter the weights" lest they be damned by the god Thoth.

In ancient China, cowry shells performed a similar role to barley in Sumer. Shell money's importance is reflected in written Chinese today: traditional characters for goods or commodities (貨), wealth (財) and buy (買), among others, all contain the radical 貝, the pictograph for shell.

Money, as its relationship with writing shows, has been an incredible force for progress and opportunity – and for cheating, fraud and social resentment. Its invention has changed the way we think about society, life and ourselves. From the start, money has been a social idea, embodied in rituals of gifts to honour rulers, gods or family elders. The personal, clan-based practice of assigning value to a gift bled into the impersonal world of commerce, in which values had to carry a different, more quantitative meaning.

Often worn round the necks of the royal family, cowrie shells soon emerged as a currency

But this story is far from linear. Humanity, having invented money about 3,000 years ago, didn't progress evenly. Money is a cultural invention, and its use varies by society. Sometimes it hit a cul-de-sac. Some societies went backwards or didn't change at all.

Ancient Egyptian civilisation extended from about 3100BCE to 30BCE, an extraordinary length of time. Throughout most of those 3,000 years, Egyptians didn't use cash or cash equivalents despite their access to vast amounts of gold and other precious metals. The idea of using shiny metal as a means of exchange or a store of value never clicked with the pharaohs (although gold was used as a unit of account; the Phoenicians used silver for the same purpose). The Egyptians reserved gold for ritual burials instead. Archaeologists today are still excavating vast treasures from the Egyptian desert.

Other societies that lacked money and markets weren't as lucky as the Egyptians. Inevitably they came into contact with more dynamic competitors. This lesson was taught in the most brutal fashion to Atahualpa, king of the Inca Empire in Peru. He began his reign high in the mists of the Andes Mountains as an absolute sovereign, owner of everything. Taxes were paid in the form of labour and the king granted subjects access to means of production, with accounts kept in the form of knotted strings.

Like the ancient Egyptians, the Incas possessed vast amounts of precious metals, which they revered. Gold was the "sweat of the sun", silver the "tears of the moon". But these were for art, religion and ritual. When in 1532 Atahualpa found himself the prisoner of the Spanish conquistador Pizarro, he agreed to a ransom of enough gold to fill the room in which he was being held, and twice that in silver. The Incas were ready to indulge Spanish avarice because they didn't understand that, to their tormenters, the shiny metal was not just a means to demonstrate power or please the gods. Atahualpa didn't appreciate that his gold and silver could be refashioned into a portable store of value and means of exchange: money.

The Incan Empire fell for multiple reasons. Disease from Europe had already ravaged the land by the time the conquistadors showed up in Cusco. The Spanish relied on superior arms, crusaders' righteousness and shameless deceit. But the Spanish also came from a culture able to project power across the oceans. They didn't rely on indentured labour to achieve this. Their rulers possessed something that Atahualpa wouldn't understand. They had access to credit.

The Incas may be forgiven for not understanding money, for they were far removed from Eurasia, where money had been in circulation for over two millennia. Yet even in the Eurasian landmass, the concept of money, or at least cash, enjoyed only a tenuous hold.

From the misty mountains of Peru, we go to the parched plains of Upper Burma. The Incas built places like Machu Picchu on a monumental scale, out of

Greedy Spanish conquistadors stunned the Aztecs and Incas with their lust for gold

stone. The medieval Burmese were avid builders, too, filling the dusty lands with beautiful temples. Today their first capital, the city of Bagan, sits on a pleasant bend of the Irrawaddy River surrounded by thousands of Buddhist pagodas.

The Bagan Empire, the kernel of modern-day Myanmar, stretched from the 9th to the 13th centuries – and it didn't use money. For four centuries, prices remained static and wealth was donated to the Buddhist church in the form of temples and monasteries to earn merit for the next life. The king was expected to donate the most, usually in the form of land, animals and labour, especially skilled artisans and engineers.

What's strange about Bagan is that the people who came before it did use money. The ancestors of the Burmese military elite were the Pyu, and they minted plenty of silver coins that were used to trade throughout the region. Bagan was founded, however, as a seat of empire that regressed to a static, inland, agrarian society in which karma, not wealth, dictated status.

All of Bagan's excess production went to building pagodas, so gradually, the Buddhist church grew rich while the king grew poor. This was fine so long as their neighbours were weak or too far away to be a threat. But being a static, feudal empire only works until it comes up against something different – as was the case for Bagan in 1287 when the Mongols came storming in. So ended both the Bagan Empire and the Burmese experiment with a moneyless society.

Most societies did, however, use commodities to serve some monetary functions. Cattle was at the centre of relationships for many Mediterranean cultures, which is why the word pecuniary, or "related to money", is derived from the Latin *pecunarius* (wealth in cattle). Similarly, the English word salary derives from the Italian *salario*, which comes from the Latin for salt. In the Americas, European colonisers used deerskins as a form of money, which is why the dollar is nicknamed the buck.

The list of these primitive forms of payment can fill pages: cowry shells for the peoples around the Indian Ocean, whale teeth for the Polynesians, cacao seeds for the Aztecs, rice for the Burmese and, oddest of all, giant stone discs on the remote island of Yap. Odd, but also sophisticated – the Yap islanders used the stones to offset credits and debts among the populace.

Cowry shells might have been prized in the Maldives, but they would have meant nothing to a Bedouin intending to trade in cows, and vice versa. Money travels only as far as people believe in it as both a means of payment and a store of intrinsic value.

Such belief is a deeply human decision, one that varies across cultures and time. Even gold and other precious metals were not universally valued as forms of money (although they were usually accorded a different value, as magical or divine). Gold could be refashioned as ingots, bars or coins, and unlike other metals, it does not tarnish. It is pure. And yet the Egyptians, Incas and Burmese – civilisations rich in the arts, astronomy and engineering – did not use it to store value or as a means of exchange (although it sometimes served as a unit of account).

Other societies did, and they discovered this gave them great power. The invention of money led to credit and modern finance. It redefined the way people value what's important in life. The invention of money first reflected ancient culture, and then changed it.

And it's still changing us. We are on the doorstep of a new culture of money. Money that is code. Money that is programmable.

This new world of cryptocurrencies has strange, regressive features. Money-as-code is now stored on little pieces of hardware and trustees arranging payments need to open a physical vault and handle these memory sticks with their hands. The passkeys required to unlock the code must be memorised or written down somewhere offline.

This system for digital cash is clumsier than the way banks treated securities in the days when stocks and bonds were still embodied as pieces of paper. At least then a bearer bond could still be used by someone as a claim if they had possession of the certificate. But there's no recourse when private keys to cryptocurrencies are hacked, forgotten or lost.

Perhaps even odder still in today's world is the overwhelming primacy of the US dollar, a currency that isn't gold, or silver, or anything at all tangible. It is pure fiat, yet it rules the world simply because we believe in it. The foreign-exchange market today trades USD6.6 trillion in volume daily, mostly in and around the dollar. Are we just fooling ourselves, or is there something more to the dollar – or to e-money – that's nothing more than strings of code?

Does it matter if money has become this intangible and disconnected from the "real world"? Is this why we keep suffering financial crises? Is there any credence to arguments that we should have a gold standard, or rely on bitcoin as the next world currency, or wait for another fiat currency like the euro or the Chinese yuan to take over? Will a change in monetary regime also change our culture, just as money has always done?

The best way to address such questions is to put them in context and understand what came before. The story of currencies is intertwined with that of civilisation.

The classic definition of civilisation is a complex society based on urban development, a system of writing and the concentration of power over people and over the natural environment. Among these ingredients, the "secret sauce" is money. It's the part that's intangible and therefore, invisible – almost.

The Sumerians and the ancient Chinese made the first links between money, writing and language. But to understand how money really turbocharged civilisation – and to catch a glimpse of what may lie in our own future – take a journey back 3,000 years to what is now Turkey. Something startling is about to happen.

Would-be tax assessors risked the wrath of Thoth if they moved the weights and measures

HOW WE LEARNED TO COUNT

Counting systems predated writing. Tallies by carving notches into wood, bone or stone go back at least 40,000 years, before the advent of agriculture. We can only guess what people were counting: days, solar or lunar cycles, numbers of animals? Here are some of the earliest known examples of written tallies.

THE LEBOMBO BONE: Made from a baboon's fibula, this bone tool was found in the Lebombo Mountains, between South Africa and Swaziland. It is around 43,000 years old and bears 29 notches. One theory suggests this was a lunar calendar for women to keep track of their menstrual cycles, suggesting women may have invented mathematics.

PERSIAN CLAY TOKENS: The earliest known writing for recordkeeping is a pair of clay tablets from Iran used to count sheep. At first they used one token for one or two sheep, but the need to count flocks led them to use tokens representing different numbers of animals. Eventually, around 4000BCE, they strung these together to form different counts and developed security measures to ensure the validity of the count, suggesting ownership and trading.

SUMERIAN CUNEIFORM: Ancient Mesopotamia had many numeric systems: one for animals, another for tools, a third for grain, and so on. Perhaps this confusion is why Sumerians invented arithmetic. Once people learned to add and subtract, say, grain, it was possible to apply this to other commodities and then begin to compare volumes. By around 2100BCE, measurements converged on a standard numbering system with 60 as its base (as opposed to 10 in our decimal system).

02
COINAGE

Sandwiched between Persia
and Greece, the Lydians
thrived as middlemen

Herodotus was born in the fifth century BCE in Halicarnassus (modern-day Bodrum, Turkey), a Hellenic city on the edges of the Persian Empire. He liked to travel, and today, he is famous for writing "The Histories", which is considered the first work of narrative history. Much of it concerns the wars between ancient Greece and Persia, but it also contains many comments and observations about the different lands he visited.

For example, consider this nugget: "They [the Lydians] were the first of men, so far as we know, who struck and used coin of gold or silver; and also they were the first retail traders."

Lydia was a kingdom in western Turkey sandwiched between the new Hellenic world and the old Persian one – so naturally, the Lydians thrived as middlemen. Their realm also included generous amounts of electrum, a naturally occurring mix of silver and gold. By itself, electrum could serve as proto-money. But Lydian merchants decided to experiment with minting coins of electrum, producing the first in the 630s BCE. They stamped them with the lion insignia of the king, thereby linking the weight of electrum in the coin with his prestige.

Other civilisations had been toying with the idea of coins. As early as the ninth century BCE, Chinese people along the Yellow River began casting bronze in the form of cowry shells – that is, making fake cowries. These may have started as stamps from the king, like an entitlement granted to loyal retainers, which could be redeemed for a service or goods. (In today's emerging world of blockchain currencies, we might call this a "utility token".)

These fake cowries then became tradable, with their value derived from being the king's token, not from the user being the king's recipient. By the Warring States period (the fifth century BCE), if not earlier, coins were cast as true money. Casting means they were formed in a mould, which allowed for precise shapes. Coins were modelled after spades or knives (also originally gift goods) and were measured by weight, although standards varied from place to place.

These Chinese coins coexisted with other variants of money, such as cloth. Chinese coins became widely used, but their impact was shallow. China's earliest dynasties still lacked retail markets, relegating coins to supplemental roles in what remained economies based on tribute.

Those markets might have emerged, but in 221 BCE the first emperor to rule over all of classical China, Qin Shihuangdi, sent China in a different direction. Shihuangdi remains arguably the most important person in Chinese history, as a centraliser and a tyrant. Among his innovations was abolition of all forms of coinage except one: a round copper coin with a square hole in the middle. Called the *ban liang*, this coin predated the Qin Dynasty but was elevated to China's standard monetary unit, a position it would retain until the 1920s.

Money is a cultural technology, not an act of nature, so its creation and use in one society differs from another's. In China, the proliferation of bronze coins came early, probably earlier than in Turkey, but their incompatibility and the lack of markets limited their impact. And when the Qin Dynasty finally did create a national standard coin, it did so more to snuff out political competition and improve tax collection. The Qin clamped down on any other changes that monetisation could bring about.

In the West, though, Lydian coinage took a far more radical turn. From the start, Lydian coins were linked to the king, although the idea probably originated with private merchants. Stamping these nuggets with kingly symbols flattened them into roundish discs, giving us the basic form of the coins we still use today. (Unlike Chinese casters, the Lydians banged a soft metal with a die and hammer, a technique that would endure in the West.) Such marks told people that the king was promising the coin contained a certain amount of electrum that was 75% gold and 25% silver.

Now famous for writing
The Histories, Herodotus
loved to travel

By minting coins in a variety of weights, the Lydians introduced fractionalisation. The basic unit of a Lydian stater (the Greek term for "coin", derived from its original meaning as "weight") was 14.1g, but the most popular denomination was one-third of a stater, which expanded the range of goods that could be traded.

They even minted coins as light as a ninety-sixth share, or 0.15g. (Early Chinese castings also came in plenty of weightings, but the Qin emperor, in his zeal for standardisation, removed these variations.)

Lydian coins circulated like wildfire, well beyond the kingdom. In today's language, coinage was the first example of financial technology – FinTech – and arguably no economic invention has ever surpassed this one.

Coinage led to huge changes in Lydian society. The most obvious was that the Lydian elite got very, very rich. By inventing coins, they also invented seigniorage: embedding a tax as the difference between the currency's face value and the cost of minting and distributing it. That trick made the king the richest man in the world.

Herodotus wrote that metallurgists working for the last of the Lydian kings, Croesus, figured out how to separate electrum's components. This allowed the king to create standardised coins in pure silver and pure gold, creating yet new tiers of values that everyone could trust. Croesus ruled from 560 to 547BCE, and even for today's tech and finance tycoons, to be "as rich as Croesus" remains a high bar.

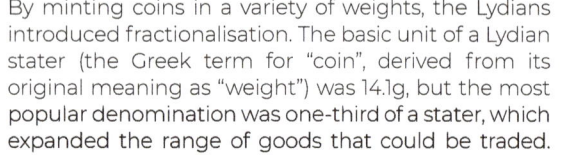

But the invention of coinage went much further: as Herodotus noted, Lydians were also the first to set up retail shops. Before this point, Lydia had prospered thanks to its bulk trade in cosmetics and perfumes, but it was otherwise self-sufficient in producing food. Just as everywhere else, its people ate what they grew and wore what they weaved. Proto-monies lacked standardisation, so their use in trade and payments was subject to haggling and metal ingots were only useful for bulk transactions.

Lydian coins eliminated uncertainty (notwithstanding the fact that the invention immediately following coinage was counterfeiting). The advent of coinage made transactions fast, convenient and credible. This, combined with the introduction of small-value silver coins, gave the general population access to money – what we'd consider today the first instance of "financial inclusion".

Commerce both great and petty took off. The speed with which retail markets sprung up suggests a huge pent-up demand for exchange that could not exist with just proto-money and brokers. Nor could trade boom when the lack of trust in proto-money (and in brokers) meant goods were only exchanged within the family or other close connections. Suddenly people didn't have to grow all of their own food or make their own clothes. Economic opportunities weren't limited to kith and kin. People could go to the town market and buy whatever they needed or sell their excess produce.

The Lydians had created more than physical tokens. They had put money into general circulation as a general medium of exchange. They had created a currency. Doing so fostered brand-new goods and services, along with new habits and behaviours. It's no coincidence that Sardis, the Lydian capital (and site of the royal mint), is where the world's first commercial brothels were established (prostitution otherwise being associated with temples). According to Herodotus, Lydians of all social ranks did a roaring trade in selling off their daughters.

Money could be used for oppression – and for liberation. Herodotus also noted (with equal alarm) that Lydian women accrued enough coins to fill their own dowries and thereby choose whom they married.

Another invention that came with the introduction of coins was gambling. Dice had existed for millennia but were probably used for fortune-telling and harmless games. The Lydians added coins to the mix. But gambling was not the only way coins encouraged the idle. Lydia's richest families also invented conspicuous consumption, lapping up luxury goods and competing to build magnificent homes and family tombs. There is no evidence, however, that they invested their wealth in anything productive. They simply blew it all.

And that wasn't just in the sense of consuming, gambling and whoring. Croesus, in what may still be the greatest rich-man's folly of all time, decided to invade the mighty Persian Empire. The Persians counterattacked and seized Sardis, where legend has it they burned Croesus and his wife on a pyre.

The Persians, having conquered Lydia, tried to adopt gold coins. But Persia remained a vast tribute state. The circulation of Persian coins was not accompanied by an explosion in private retail trade. Money is a cultural technology and some cultures, such as ancient China and Persia, chose to apply the brakes. Coins alone weren't enough to transform society; they had to be allowed to circulate freely, through retail markets. Had the fate of coinage remained in Persian hands, the revolutionary changes it wrought would have been snuffed out.

But the true inheritors of Lydia's coinage were its neighbours to the west: the young civilisation of the Greeks. Rather than an empire built on tribute, they were a patchwork of squabbling, independent city-states – a noisy rabble on the fringes of civilisation.

What they were about to do with money would astonish the world.

Croesus was doomed after deciding to invade the mighty Persian Empire

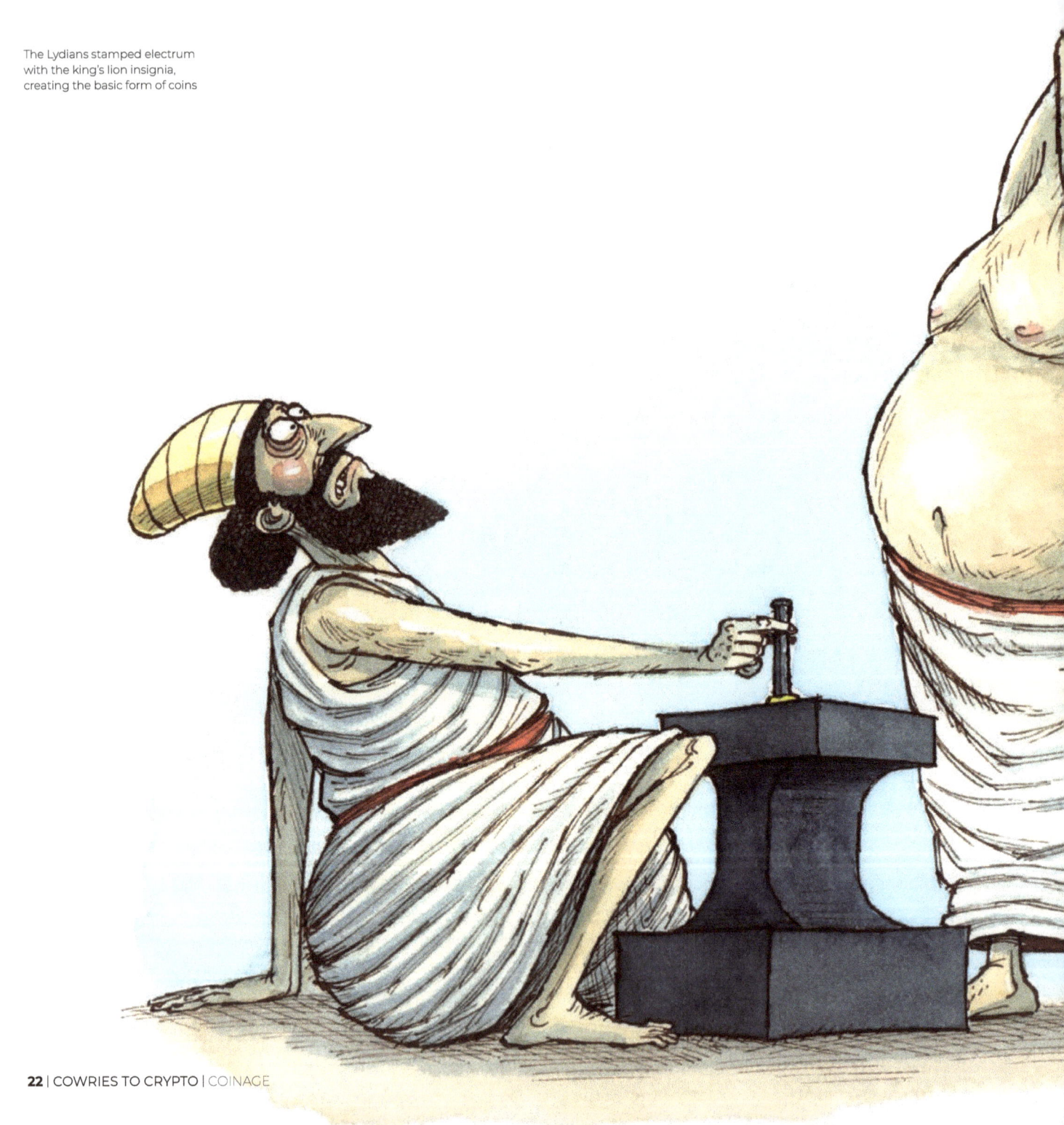

The Lydians stamped electrum with the king's lion insignia, creating the basic form of coins

FAMOUS COINS

HERE ARE ACCOUNTS OF SEVERAL NOTABLE COINS, BASED ON THE WEBSITE FLEUR-DE-COIN.COM

THE OLDEST COIN in the world is the earliest known Lydian one-sixth stater dating back 2,700 years. It was struck in Efesos, a Hellenic city on the coast of Asia Minor. Hand struck, it features a design on only one side, a lion's head; there is a punch mark on the reverse. This coin is on exhibit at the British Museum's department of coins and medals.

For a time, **THE MOST VALUABLE COIN** in the world was a twenty-dollar Double Eagle made of gold ore minted in 1933, the year the government stopped producing these. President Franklin Delano Roosevelt had banned private payments or hoarding of gold, having just taken the depression-struck country off the gold standard. The last batch made was never issued; the coins were destroyed – except one, stolen by the Federal Mint's chief cashier, who somehow sold it to Egypt's King Farouk, a collector.

Farouk refused to give it back to the US (which regarded it as stolen property), a position retained by the Egyptian government after the king died. The coin's whereabouts became a mystery until 1996, when an English coin dealer tried to sell it to an American collector at the Waldorf-Astoria Hotel in New York. The dealer was arrested, but sued. While the case wound through the courts, the coin was kept in a vault at the World Trade Center. It was briefly lost again in the 2001 terrorist attacks that felled the Twin Towers, but then recovered and moved to Fort Knox. The US and the English dealer finally settled out of court, with the US allowing the Double Eagle to be privately owned. An anonymous bidder in 2002 won the coin at a Sotheby's auction for USD7,590,020.

However, in 2013, an anonymous buyer purchased a single US silver dollar for USD10m. Why? Its beautiful depiction of Lady Liberty with flowing locks wasn't the main reason. This was the first ever coin minted by the Federal Mint, in 1794, and according to broker Stacks & Bowers, that was enough to make it worth ten million bucks – and the most valuable coin to date.

THE FIRST COIN in the world stamped with a QR code was issued in 2011 by the Royal Dutch Mint to celebrate the Utrecht-based mint's 100th anniversary. The coins come in silver and gold editions in EUR5 and EUR10 denominations. The QR code directs you to the mint's website at www.q5g.nl/en

03
TRANSFORMATION

From Plato to Aristotle,
philosophers failed to agree
on the concept of money

The Persian Empire discovered coinage when it conquered Lydia in 546BCE. But currency had little impact in Persia, which was a vast tribute state ruled by a centralised military. The Persians never built new mints in their Iranian homeland. They relied on the Lydian mints at Sardis.

At first the Persians churned out more Croeseids (coins in the style set out by Croesus), until their emperor Darius told the mint to issue gold coins with his likeness. It was the first time coins would bear a person's portrait. These gold Daric coins became a local standard.

But much to Darius's confusion, most coins circulating throughout the Persian realm were silver units – from Greece.

And whereas the Persians relied solely on one or two mints in Sardis, the Greek coins were stamped with symbols from more than 30 different cities. It wasn't that a particular Greek mint, under the command of a single king, had become internationally popular. They all had.

Persia was a mighty empire and Greece was a strange outlier of quarrelling city-states. How had Persia's monetary system become Greek, under the noses of all-powerful rulers such as Darius?

Greek civilisation had been around for a long time – the Trojan War probably took place in the 12th century BCE. But it had always existed apart from the great empires that dominated the world, such as Egypt, Babylon and Persia.

Greece itself was a rugged land of mountains that lent itself to fragmentation. Here developed a collection of tiny, independent cities that spent most of their time fighting one another.

Their cultural claim to fame at this point was the alphabet, another technology that fuelled works such as Homer's "Iliad". There were budding signs of greatness in this strange, dynamic world. But the great achievements of Greek civilisation were yet to come. It needed a catalyst.

Once Hellenic towns in Asia Minor adopted Lydian coinage, this new technology spread quickly through the Aegean and to the leading cities on the Greek mainland. In its wake emerged a brand-new way of running a society.

Coinage propelled Greek culture into the role of the breakout civilisation of the West.

COINS, POLITICS AND LAW

Nowhere was this truer than in Athens. This city had the good fortune to be about 50km from silver mines at Laurion. As the Athenians learned to isolate silver ore and strike coins, a market economy took off.

The tributary empires of Egypt and Asia relied on a competent bureaucracy and recordkeeping to levy taxes and coordinate long-distance transfers of wheat and other goods.

But money in the form of coins eliminated the need for administrators or police to manage transactions. Moreover, money opened the possibility of exchange to a broader section of society. Coins were anonymous – the user had to trust the money, not the other person. In today's jargon, coins "democratised finance" and the agora (market) became a unique feature of Greek communities. Money and markets chiselled away at the traditional bonds of kinship – and political power.

The Greeks didn't create markets out of thin air. Those foundations had already been laid as money was just entering the culture. Solon, the wise lawmaker of Athens (died circa 560BCE), lived at a time when coinage was widespread among the Hellenic cities of Asia Minor and the nearby island of Aegina, but had yet to spread to Athens, which was still a land of farmers. Change was in the air, however, and Solon was part of that movement.

Early bankers were little more than money lenders and loan sharks, quick to resort to violence

On the political front, Solon threw open membership in the city's Assembly to people of wealth, not just the sons of the existing oligarchs. In the economic realm, he standardised weights and measures. He pursued other reforms that lent the city, in these formative years, a culture of civic-mindedness and frugality.

Greek democracy arose in Athens and other cities that had adopted coinage, the agora and the principles of citizenship. Indeed, the Greek word for coinage, *nomisma*, comes from their word for law, *nomos*. From this also comes the English word numismatic, relating to the study or collection of currency.

Not all cities took the money route. Sparta, notably, resisted coins and the market economy, favouring a militarised society based on slave labour instead. Other Greek cities also relied on slaves (the miners of Laurion were slaves of Athenians). But many Athenian citizens worked in the agora. In its early years, Athens was a proud city of artisans, manufacturers and shopkeepers – and bankers.

The world's first known financier was Pythius, who lived in Asia Minor and became obscenely rich. Corinth was home to Philostephanus who, in the early fifth century BCE, banked the wealth of Themistocles, the first populist to be elected ruler of Athens.

The most celebrated banker was Pasion (before 430BCE to 370CE), who came to Athens as a foreign slave. He worked as a scribe for local moneychangers and was so talented that they granted him his freedom and eventually their bank. Pasion was eventually named a citizen of Athens. He died an incredibly wealthy man, handing over his affairs to Phormio, another brilliant slave-turned-banker.

Banking is a fancy word for what people like Philostephanus and Pasion did, which was a combination of loan-sharking and making markets in different types of coins while also protecting their customers from being cheated by counterfeits.

Financiers (including temple priests) used this primitive version of foreign-exchange trading to get into higher-risk, higher-reward lines of work, such as lending to merchants and shipmasters. All of this was conducted via coins. And they also accepted deposits from clients, who ranged from ordinary businessmen to statesmen such as Themistocles.

Interestingly, these proto-banks did not pay interest on deposits, which clients valued as a service for safekeeping (or keeping valuables away from the tax collector's gaze). Banks only charged interest on deposits they could lend to other clients; this was such a high-risk business that banks didn't dare use their own capital.

Wealth was not limited to just a few moneychangers and merchants. Many citizens prospered, eroding the power of aristocratic families in favour of merchants and shopkeepers. This allowed citizens to enjoy leisure. Finance, underpinned by sound money, supported the development of Greek drama, philosophy, science and art.

And more, a society that became based on money – on counting, on calculated decisions – supported a totally different way of thinking about the world, one that was more abstract and less personal. Inquiries into the nature of life and the university began to hinge on reason and less on the whims of the gods.

One of the things the great philosophers argued over, of course, was money. Plato, who equated wealth with corruption, wanted to outlaw metallic coins and replace them with government-issued tokens for the single purpose of recordkeeping. He would have found much to admire in Lenin's Russia.

Aristotle, on the other hand, argued for private property and the need to manage wealth. He praised stamped coins for their convenience, although he didn't understand their anonymous nature. He thought prices should be determined by the social status of the participants, not the value of the merchandise.

As a result, there was a tension between philosophers and money from the start. This was partly because thoughtful people couldn't ignore the divergence of fortunes that money wrought, but the conflict goes deeper. Philosophers were from the aristocracy; men of money were self-made, even former slaves, who could challenge the ruling order because they had amassed more coins than other people. The authority of rulers was expressed in the form of gifts or payments to favoured loyalists, but in the agora, people didn't need the favour of aristocrats to benefit from exchange.

Eventually, intellectuals took a more practical approach to money. Xenophon wrote a book describing, in part, how to manage the finances of an estate, a skill he called *oikonomikos* (economics). Aristotle also praised *oikonomikos* as a path towards man's virtue, provided it wasn't subverted into greed for money's own sake.

But it was Herodotus's observations of politics and warfare, not the enquiries of philosophers, that identified the link between coins and markets. Where money was concerned, real-world power was always at stake.

MONEY, POWER AND WAR

The Athenian state used coins to pay people for jury service or attending the Assembly, but most of all it used them to finance its navy. Athens, with its Laurion supply and military might, saw its silver drachma become the most important among a monetary system of competing Greek currencies.

At first Athens strove to be the dominant city-state in the Hellenic world, but a new threat loomed. After swallowing Lydia, Persia went on to conquer the Greek cities along the coast of Asia Minor. The Persians were keen to stamp out the feisty, independent ways of these new acquisitions, but the local tyrants they installed among the Ionian cities only sparked rebellion. And when Athens used its money, and its navy, to come to the aid of the rebels, the Persians turned the full might of their army towards the destruction of Greece as a whole.

The Persians launched a vast invasion in 480BCE. A land attack met with success and needed only to be joined by an even bigger Persian army being transported across the Aegean.

But the Persians were outmatched at sea by a combined Greek fleet led by Themistocles at the Battle of Salamis – a fleet representing many cities, unified by the foreign threat, but largely financed by Laurion silver. A Persian victory would have probably strangled the development of Greek civilisation, making this battle one of the most significant in Western history.

Eventually the Greeks went on the offensive. More than 300 cities joined to free Ionia from Persia's grasp. This alliance was called the Delian League, named after the island of Delos.

Delos was a barren rock that surprisingly became Athens's greatest commercial competitor. Long a centre of cult worship (it was said to be the birthplace of the gods Apollo and Artemis), it became universally accepted as neutral ground, first for religion and then for trade. This made it the logical venue to store the League's treasure, turning Delos into something like an offshore financial centre, a sort of Hong Kong for the ancient Mediterranean. Delos attracted merchants from across Greece and abroad, even from a rising power in Italy called Rome. Delian moneychangers ran the treasure vault as a bank, putting themselves in the middle of trades as neutral guarantors. This was a service that presaged the modern clearing house.

This "Bank of Delos" created the financing required for little Greece to defeat giant Persia. The outcome was more than the story of a Goliath felled by a David. It was the first instance of a centralised tributary system being overwhelmed by a commercial culture powered by markets and money.

Success bred hubris, however. Athens at its zenith had lost its spirit of frugal citizens in the agora. This new generation had become snobs who felt labour was fit only for slaves. Athens grew equally high-handed about its place in the world. It bent the Delian fleet to its own purposes and turned its mercantile links into a coercive empire. This alienated smaller city-states, especially Sparta. The seeds of another conflict were sown. The Peloponnesian War destroyed Athens, while Sparta emerged victorious thanks in part to a huge subsidy in gold given it by a vengeful Persia.

Were Sparta's victory the end of the matter, the story of money might have been subdued. The Greek experiment in coins, markets and democracy could have become a mere footnote, and coinage taken on the minor role given it elsewhere. But a new dynamic was set to take Greek-style money global.

Alexander was about to become Great.

MOST VALUABLE COINS OF ANCIENT GREECE

According to www.coinarchives.com, the following are some of the rarest, most valuable coins from ancient Lydia and Greece that have sold recently in auctions.

LYDIAN KINGDOM: A stater from the reign of Croesus sold on January 6th 2019 for USD80,000. Struck at Sardis in 553-539BCE, it portrays a lion raising its paw on one side and a bull on the reverse. It is made in the "light" standard, meaning it is electrum deliberately made with less gold content, only 54% (and 44% silver). Croesus's father reputedly debased his electrum coins, which were supposed to be 75% gold. The government recalled the debased coins and reissued these staters that matched the actual portions – so that users got "what it says on the tin". These coins are fragile and therefore rare. Reportedly, a buyer acquired a similar coin through a Japanese auction house recently for USD180,000.

ATHENS: On May 6th 2019, an Athenian decadrachm sold for SFr650,000 (USD638,695). The decadrachm was a large silver coin, and this one portrays Athena in profile, wearing a crested helmet, with her owl, wings spread, on the reverse. Made in the 460s BCE, these coins are among the most prestigious Greek coins for collectors, partly because of the debate about their purpose. Herodotus said this denomination was used to pay citizens for surpluses from the silver mines at Laurion; if so, this one may have been issued to commemorate the Greek victory over the Persians at the Battle of Marathon in 490BCE. There is debate as to whether this denomination was used as common currency.

Much like David and Goliath, Greece felled the mighty Persia, despite being heavily outnumbered

04
IMPERIUM

Having declared himself dictator for life,
Caesar was assassinated by senators
hoping to preserve the Republic

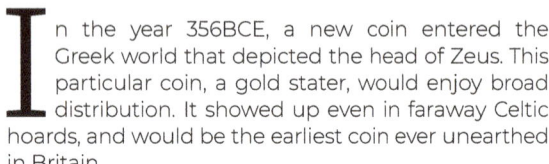

In the year 356BCE, a new coin entered the Greek world that depicted the head of Zeus. This particular coin, a gold stater, would enjoy broad distribution. It showed up even in faraway Celtic hoards, and would be the earliest coin ever unearthed in Britain.

But there was something else about this coin. Many people confused its portrait of Zeus with its likeness to the man who commanded its creation: Philip II of Macedonia.

Greek coins depicted gods or symbols of the city, usually with an inscription stating where the coin was minted. Coins were thus used to promote city-states and connect them with a divine patron. Kingly images were for Asian despots like the Persians, not for the free citizens of democratic Greece.

Philip struck his gold coin to commemorate his racehorse's victory in the Olympics. (This was also the year his wife gave birth to his son, Alexander.) If the image of Zeus just happened to resemble him, a move viewed by Greeks as crass, well, who was he to object?

Greeks' disdain for Macedonia blinded them to Philip's military capabilities. His gold stater with its Zeus profile was his way of telling the world he had arrived. Minting coins was also necessary to planning for war. He improved upon the Greek phalanx (tight formations of spearmen) with flanking cavalry, a combination that devastated Athenian and Theban rivals. Soon most of Classical Greece lay at Philip's feet, but this was just stage one: Philip planned to attack Persia. The Asian campaign would be expensive. Thanks to nearby gold mines in the Macedonian mountains, he had the means to pay for it. He began producing money at a furious rate.

Philip brought Greece to heel, but he was assassinated before he could march east. Young Alexander assumed the throne at age 20 and turned out to be an even more ambitious commander. For one thing, he would not be content with disguising his image as a god: his coins would be adorned with his beautiful visage. Alexander, after all, believed he was a deity, one destined to rule over the entire world.

And so began the new age of world empire, enabled by coinage. Philip had intended to simply free the Greek cities of Asia Minor and perhaps conquer Anatolia. That was not nearly enough for Alexander. For the next ten years, starting in 334BCE, he would wage conquest upon conquest, forging a realm from the Adriatic Sea to the Punjab (and connected economically to Greek trading settlements as far west as Gibraltar).

The world had seen its share of empires, but none like this. No other was so great in its extent, nor in its merging of the Greek and Asian worlds, nor in the way its leader used coins to knit it together.

He paid his army cash; so too the artists and engineers in his train. He activated the local mint in each new land to produce more coins bearing his likeness. To ensure Alexandrian money would circulate throughout, he ordained standard weights, designs and a simple conversion: ten pieces of silver for one gold coin.

Alexander understood that the person who writes the rules for money wields power.

He founded 70 or more new towns and cities across North Africa and West and South Asia, populating them with Greek generals and their families – all of whom used newly minted coins to jump-start local market economies.

In short, Alexander exported the Greek money-based culture to most of the known world (except China), while harnessing coins for the service of his personality cult.

Alexander died in Babylon in 323BCE and his empire collapsed instantly, carved into kingdoms ruled by his various generals and satraps. But his monetary system endured in Asia and in the rising power to the west, Rome.

Founded in 753 BCE, the city of Rome relied on heads of cattle as currency for many years

ROME: REPUBLIC TO EMPIRE

The Roman republic was slow to adopt money despite having contact with Greek settlements in southern Italy and Sicily. But Roman merchants at Delos had absorbed the lessons of coinage. They witnessed what a sound financial system could do to generate wealth and finance the army.

Eventually coinage and private markets became the financial basis of the new Roman world. Had Rome not embraced money as the organising driver of society, it likely would never have gotten so big, nor endured for so long. But the beginning of Roman coinage was fitful.

The city of Rome was founded in 753BCE, but for a long time it relied on heads of cattle as units of account. This was fine for subduing the Italian peninsula, but there was no way proto-money could finance foreign wars or integrate overseas lands into Roman markets.

The Republic struck its first silver coin in 269BCE to fund the Punic Wars against Carthage. The basic unit was a silver coin called the denarius, originally worth ten asses. This was too much to pay soldiers, so the most common coin became the low-value sestertius. The Republic struggled to maintain the integrity of the denarius and frequently ran out of cash, forcing the rulers to rely on borrowing (from senators and other wealthy people engaged in private lending). This encouraged currency reform and the issuance of new, higher-value denominations such as the gold aureus. These kept a steady value over the next 200 years, through the Republic's transition into Empire.

Although many cities in the Roman realm minted their own coins, the centre of the action was the Temple of Juno Moneta on the Capitoline Hill, overlooking the Roman Forum. The temple itself served as a vault, fusing finance with Roman religion.

Juno Moneta was the object of a cult throughout the Roman world. Her name, Moneta, was derived from the Latin *monere* (to warn). She was the patroness of the city, whose job was to alert the rulers to instability. At first her job was to warn of invaders, but she quickly morphed into the guardian of the city's funds. From her name, of course, we have derived the English words money and mint (although the Romans used the term *pecunia* for money).

And from her temple spewed lots and lots of denarii. The mint at Juno Moneta was a non-stop operation, so much so that our modern word currency is derived from the Latin *currere* (to flow, to run – in other words, to circulate).

By the second century BCE, Rome was awash with unprecedented wealth. This came primarily from exploiting mines in conquered lands, emptying them of their gold and other commodities, as well as from minting money. The Roman monetary system, building on the Greek, penetrated the entire known world except for China. The ubiquity of coins assimilated new territories into the empire and extended the market economy of private trade, a process usually initiated by paying Rome's conquering centurions in cash.

The vast spoils sparked civil wars among generals vying to amass these riches. Money was literally power, and without civic checks on warlords such as Julius Caesar, the Republic could not last. Caesar, after declaring himself dictator for life, was assassinated by senators hoping to preserve the Republic. But his successor Octavian was anointed with the title Augustus in 27 BCE, thus becoming the first emperor, Caesar Augustus. Octavian issued a gold coin in his image that affirmed both monetary integrity and his imperium (absolute power).

Since the time of Alexander, vast conquests led to the expansion of market-based trade. Roman coins bound far-flung lands together in commercial and administrative networks. Within the empire, the Pax Romana allowed private markets to set prices and enrich the elite. The Empire grew in prosperity for nearly 200 years.

But whereas Greece had used money to expand a productive market-based economy, Rome's growth proved unsustainable because it was based on tribute rather than productivity. The markets established by Roman coin were mostly overseas; the city of Rome didn't produce much of anything. For many in Italy, quality of life was high, but the elite spent their wealth on luxuries, particularly from Asia, or on land speculation. This led to a constant drain of gold and silver to foreign, often hostile, lands.

More and more of the government's funds, meanwhile, went to the burgeoning bureaucracy and the army, despite that it was bringing back less and less plunder. The rest of the funds went to feeding and diverting the Roman mob ("bread and circuses").

No one bothered to invest in industry. But the printing machine of Juno Moneta never stopped, and gradually the circulation of currency, instead of supporting a growing economy, turned inflationary.

The Temple of Juno Moneta
served as a vault, fusing finance
with Roman religion

Thinking nobody would notice, Nero reduced the silver content in coins, debasing the denarius

DECREE AND DEBASEMENT

It didn't take long for the emperors to begin messing with the currency in an attempt to keep the good times rolling. Nero, in the year 64CE, thinking no one would notice, cut back on the silver content of the denarius. He set a pattern that would continue for the next 200 years, in which each emperor engaged in debasement. The denarius, the bedrock of small-value money, started as nearly 100% silver. By the third century, Juno Moneta was producing coins made of as little as 4% silver, and other mints conjured them with virtually none.

Initially this led to mild inflation, but conditions grew chaotic. The emperors maintained the value of the gold aureus, but the constant minting of debased bronze and silver coins – the money used by the general population – led to catastrophic conditions for more and more people. The emperors insisted that taxes remain valued against the gold coins. Commoners, stuck with debased silver denarii, lost claim to their farms and sold themselves into slavery. The money economy began to regress to barter. The commercial relationships that had held the vast empire together began losing their glue.

Some perspective is called for, however. Nero is infamous for literally fiddling while Rome burned, so naturally the history books also condemn him for fiddling with the currency. But in this, Nero was perhaps more of a seer than a fool. He, or his advisors, grasped something about money that others had not: that it did not have to be purely linked to metal because it was not mere bullion, but a symbol of the emperor's power.

In other words, it was the first move towards currency by decree – by fiat, Latin for "let it be done". And the strategy worked for 200 years, for it was not until the third century that Rome fell into monetary crisis. For a long time, Rome maintained a stable monetary supply that could meet the empire's needs regardless of the whims of geology and mining. Eventually, of course, the debasement was complete, initiating a disaster intertwined with the crumbling of the empire's borders. But Nero's experiment would be repeated (if the lessons of debasement were not quite remembered) long after the fall of the Roman Empire.

In the meantime, however, third-century emperors realised they could not defend the empire's frontiers or maintain the loyalty of their armies if the currency was not rescued.

The emperor Diocletian (ruled 284-305CE) bowed to reality and split control of the empire in two, coordinated between rulers in Rome and himself in Byzantium. He also introduced the world's first government budget, which gave the administration a holistic view of taxes and expenditures.

Although Diocletian had an unprecedented view of the Roman economy, the news was bad and he lacked the levers to fix it. He tried to reform the currency with a new, pure gold coin called the solidus, but only the rich could use it. He effectively "floated" the price of gold from other currencies and inflation ran wild in copper and silver coins, further impoverishing the masses.

This was an early example of Gresham's Law, named after Thomas Gresham, an English financier in the 16th century. Gresham observed that bad money drives out good: when two forms of money circulate with the same face value, people hoard the more valuable version and it disappears, leaving only the less valuable money available. Gresham defined "good" money as commodity money whose value tracks the value of the underlying metal, and "bad" money as debased.

In 301 Diocletian, confused as to why only bad money continued to circulate, issued the Edict of Prices, dictating what goods and services were worth. He also forbade farmers from selling their land. But like all other price controls, this attempt failed. Meanwhile, farmers continued to fall into debt. Unable to pay taxes with their debased coins, they submitted to indentured servitude, which bound them to their land, thus setting the stage for feudalism.

Diocletian's successor Constantine the Great (306-337CE) was out of options. His empire was no longer a dynamo based on market forces. It had become a state-run patronage machine running out of loot. He turned to the one place left to find gold and silver: the pagan temples such as Juno Moneta. His conversion to Christianity was not entirely an act of faith. It was also one of calculation, and his armies quickly set to plundering the last source of bullion.

This prolonged the life of the empire in the east, supported by Constantine's striking a new gold solidus, standardised at 72 solidi to the Roman pound, a number easily subdivided into smaller denominations. This solidus would remain the eastern Mediterranean's standard currency for another 700 years, surviving beyond even the life of the Byzantine Empire as the model for the Arab dinar.

Things were different in the West, however, where the collapse of money destroyed civic institutions and the fabric of society. Human activity leaked out of the cities into country estates, which had to become self-sufficient instead of relying on markets. Payments, even taxes, became in kind, not cash, further tying poor people to the land. Wealthy aristocrats and the Christian Church hoarded gold and silver coins rather than allowing them to circulate.

Even before barbarians overran the Western empire in the fifth century, the urban, moneyed culture of classical Rome had been inflated away. Roman achievements in areas such as law were abandoned. The empire had been built on coinage, but Europeans forgot how to use coins. Some barbarian successor kings continued to mint crude versions of Roman coinage (the Franks would establish what became the system of pounds, shillings and pennies). But anything of value ended up in hoards, while the market was flooded with otherwise valueless coins. Some places, such as Britain, lost coinage altogether. The Dark Ages began with the removal of money from circulation.

Greece's Philip and Alexander had built world-straddling empires on the back of access to gold and silver; Rome would follow suit on a breathtaking scale. Money was directly linked to the emperor, for whom stamping coins with his likeness was paramount to asserting his authority. But when the loot ran dry, the emperors turned to debasement, with disastrous consequences.

The volume of coins in circulation peaked in the last centuries of the Western empire. It would be more than 1,000 years before money would play such a major role in Europe – or before living standards would return to what Italians had enjoyed. After the disappearance of the silver denarius, Europe would not be organised around a single currency until the advent of the euro in 1999.

This was not, however, the end of the story of money. The Romans perfected money as a tool of earthly power. Other civilisations were about to use it for altogether different purposes.

MOST VALUABLE COINS
OF THE IMPERIUM

According to www.coinarchives.com, the following are some of the rarest, most valuable coins from ancient empires that have sold at auction recently.

Greece: On May 6th 2019, a two-shekel **"PORUS MEDALLION"** from Alexander the Great sold for SFr70,000 (USD68,783). Struck in Babylon around 327BCE, it portrays an Indian archer on one side (the obverse, or "heads" side of a coin) and an elephant on the reverse. The coin was probably made as a commemorative piece for someone in Alexander's empire following the conquest of the Punjabi king Porus. Although his arrows and elephants terrified the Greeks, they won the battle at great cost. Alexander so admired Porus that he appointed him local satrap.

Rome: On January 6th 2019, a buyer paid USD70,000 for a **"SEPTIMIUS SEVERUS"**, aka the "African emperor" aureus (gold coin). This emperor ruled from 193 to 211BCE, a period of prosperity and expansion. His reign was known for producing coins portraying the imperial family. This coin has Severus on the obverse and a scene with his mother and two brothers on the reverse. The smiling family issues a message of stability, but after Severus's death, the brothers' struggle for power nearly ripped the empire apart.

Judea: On January 8th 2019, a silver shekel from the independent province of Judea sold at auction for USD46,000. It was coined in the year 70, towards the end of the Jewish War resisting Roman occupation. Within four months of its creation, the Roman emperor Titus had conquered Jerusalem and destroyed the temple. Yet Jews continued to strike silver coins in order to pay the temple's half-silver tax. Some of these rare coins were also found at Masada, the mountain stronghold where the Jews famously held out against the Romans for another three years. Most coins were then melted down for their silver value, making this **"YEAR 5 SHEKEL OF ISRAEL"** very rare. It portrays a ritual chalice and a sprig of three pomegranates.

05
FAITH

While primitive societies viewed life as cyclical, Buddhism implied a linear history

For the next thousand years, Asia would play the decisive role in culture, politics, trade, religion, art – and money. Financial innovation went hand in hand with trade, of course, but also with the birth and expansion of world religions: symbiotically with Buddhism, contentiously with Christianity and creatively with Islam.

Of these world faiths, Buddhism is the oldest. The historical Buddha lived in the fifth century BCE. (Buddhism and Hinduism both have roots in a much more ancient religion based on scriptures known as the Vedas.)

The first coins from India were even older, having emerged about a hundred years earlier, with designs that included religious symbols along with depictions of animals, agriculture or simple geometric patterns. They called these coins *karshapana*, a term that would one day evolve into the word cash.

Money didn't really take off in northern India, however, until Alexander's conquests infused it with a coin-based economy. Alexander himself died in 323BCE in Babylon, and the Asian kingdoms established by his Greek generals proved short-lived. But Greek coins would come to dominate the economies of western and southern Asia.

As Europe collapsed into the Dark Ages, abandoning both its cities and its coins for agricultural feudalism, India took over as the world's economic engine. Its kingdoms were blessed with an abundance of rice, sugar and cotton. Its cities boasted a cosmopolitan elite making advances in fields such as mathematics. For example, the first text known to reference zero and its role in decimal systems was the "Lokavibhaga", published in 458CE by a monk of the Jain religion.

BUDDHISM

What marked Buddhism as a world religion was, in part, the way it implied a linear history. Primitive societies viewed life as circular, following the rising and setting of the sun and the moon and the eternal cycle of seasons. Buddhism taught that there could be an end destination: enlightenment. Gradually this led to the notion that the future could be different from the past – and that one could prepare for it. Following the sutras created in believers the mental shift required to introduce ideas such as savings, investing and credit. Trading money today for more money tomorrow was like praying today or making charity donations to store up karma for the next life.

Buddhism was also tolerant. Buddha stressed both the inevitability of suffering for all living beings and the innate ability of us all, princes and paupers alike, to achieve enlightenment. This inclusiveness allowed Buddhism both to travel well and to accept relationships outside of one's kin – a feature that could be applied to commercial as well as religious ends. Merchants became the religion's greatest supporters, in turn helping support the spread of monasteries. Monasteries, in turn, became centres of saving and lending, as a material parallel to their more spiritual investments.

Trade and Buddhist pilgrimage routes became intertwined. Whereas Christian monasteries in Europe relied on feudal landholdings to generate income, their Buddhist counterparts acted more as quasi-banks, raising alms and then lending money or grain, and earning royalties from the monks' direct business operations, from flour mills to hydraulic oil presses.

For a religion to gain traction, it needed more than just the support of commoners. It also required the patronage and protection of kings. Rulers, however, had little interest in Buddhism, which (unlike Hinduism) had nothing to say about court rituals or earthly power. There was one important exception: Ashoka Maurya.

Ashoka's father had founded the Maurya empire (322-185BCE) out of the wreckage of the Greek invasion of India. Ashoka would go on to conquer virtually all South

Asia. Appalled by the violence his campaigns wrought, however, he converted to Buddhism.

The Mauryas were more than conquerors. They were interested in the art of good government, including coinage. The chief minister to Ashoka's father, a man named Kautilya, wrote a manual on statecraft called the *"Arthashastra"*, or "The Science of Material Gain", in which he advised the king to strike coins to earn income. This would support a bureaucracy and standing army as well as promote and tax foreign trade. The *"Arthashastra"* went so far as to suggest salary levels for everyone involved in palace affairs, from the prime minister down to the servants.

Given this interest in money and commerce, it's not surprising that Ashoka lent his patronage to a religion that was friendly to business. Perhaps remorse over his military campaigns was not the only reason behind Ashoka's Buddhism.

Although the Maurya Empire crumbled after Ashoka's passing, coinage (indigenous, Greek, Roman, Persian and Byzantine) spread along with commerce and growth. It helped turn South Asia into a wealthy network of mercantile cities and productive farmland, connected by increasingly sophisticated financial tools from lending to venture capital.

With prosperity, however, came inequality, debt and strife – the very conditions that Buddha had sought to overcome so many centuries before. Callous rulers of old could ignore these problems, but not a Buddhist king.

The *"Arthashastra"* argued that a good king should use his wealth to bring prosperity to his subjects:

"As between violation of property and physical injury, violation of property is worse," say the followers of Parashara. "Spiritual good and pleasures are rooted in money, and the world is tied up with money. Its destruction is a greater evil."

"No," says Kautilya. "Even for a very large sum of money, no one would desire the loss of life."

Under Ashoka, addressing the social consequences of money would be recast as the duty of a good Buddhist king. But passages in the *"Arthashastra"* suggest a reality in which money meant power, possibly even impunity.

THE MORALITY OF DEBT

The destructive power of greed is as old as civilisation. The first written records from Mesopotamia outlined terms for loans in which defaults often led to destitution and slavery – a pattern repeated in Greece and Rome. The use of money to facilitate barter led immediately to both savings and to debt, to haves and have-nots. It also led to the need to find a way for societies to tame finance, lest it trigger rebellion.

The Mesopotamians, lacking coins, developed a sophisticated banking system, and their rulers also responded with legal measures to uphold the system while limiting the worst impact on the vulnerable. The most famous of these is the Code of Hammurabi, issued around 1754BCE.

Most of the king's edict deals with wages, contracts and liabilities. Although penalties for defaulting on a debt were harsh, Hammurabi's Code also sets limits, such as putting a three-year moratorium on indentured service. Later statesmen in other countries would revisit such tensions. Solon of Greece abolished debt-related bondage and mandated debt forgiveness – measures that didn't stick.

More sophisticated religions evolved partly in response to such pressures. The historical Buddha was born an urban prince who as a young man was shocked by the suffering he witnessed. His solution was to renounce all desire and extinguish one's ego. Although Buddha wanted his followers to abandon worldly things, his faith was based on the notion that ultimate salvation depended on a person's adherence to best practices, gained over many rebirths, rather than on their earthly social status.

This belief reinforced market-inspired notions of interacting with people other than kin and accumulating merit. And while Buddha had turned his back on the concept of princely birthright, he had also rejected asceticism suffered for its own sake. He sought the Middle Path.

These ideas came to be interpreted to suggest that one's merit could be reflected in their accumulated wealth. (If good acts in the past life were to be rewarded in the next, then someone born rich must have been a good Buddhist in the previous cycle.)

This is of course a perversion of Buddha's teachings, but it became embedded in Buddhist cultures, perhaps to encourage donations to monasteries. Anyway, following Buddha's precepts to the letter was nigh impossible. It was far easier to achieve merit through donation. From there, it was a simple step to finding merit in the act of accumulating wealth itself.

Buddhist pilgrimage trails evolved in tandem with the emergence of the Silk Road. Buddhism's biggest impact would not be felt in India, where after Ashoka, for lack of further royal patronage, it gradually lost ground to Hinduism. Rather, its biggest role would be in its export to Central Asia, the Himalayas, Southeast Asia and especially China (and from there to Korea and Japan).

The Chinese Sui and Tang dynasties (together from 581 to 907) deepened trade networks into Central Asia using caravans of camels. The Silk Road became a roadway for Buddhism too, but China imported more than just its teachings. With Buddhism came other Indian imports of a more commercial design, based around Buddhist monasteries: auctions, compound interest, equitable mortgages and money as risk capital.

Until this point, China had developed its own system of coinage independent of the Mediterranean world. But rulers restricted money to paying taxes, and there was little in the way of credit, which usually took the form of forced loans to the emperor, disguised as charity.

Markets and coins were widespread but shallow. Most people lived on subsistence agriculture, and government tribute determined trade. As in pre-Buddhist India, mindsets were circular; only the elite engaged in ancestor worship, which implied a linear story.

The arrival of Buddhism, though resisted by many inside China, connected the country to the rest of the world, helping supercharge it into *the* global economic and cultural dynamo. Gradually markets began to supersede government tribute, credit was extended to industry and innovation, and bureaucrats were paid in cash. China would soon repay the favour with financial innovations of its own – a topic for later.

If Buddhism was an old religion being retooled into a driver of financial innovation, then Islam was a new religion that would spur even more radical change – but it would do so against the odds, for Islam had a difficult relationship with money.

Both Buddhism and Islam, and the fusion of their pilgrimage and trade networks, helped connect Asia and the Middle East in an overlapping economy. From about 500 to 1500, these routes facilitated a busy trade in science, religion, art, scholarship and commerce, linking the China centric world of East Asia with the mountains and oases of central Asia and Turkey, the Indian world and the communities of Islam, which penetrated Africa and incorporated Muslim Spain.

This vast and diverse region adopted some common norms. One was the awarding of silk robes at court, a ritual that was practiced from Beijing to Baghdad. These public ceremonies established relationships between givers and recipients, greasing political, religious and commercial relationships.

Trade networks were not national, however. Merchants didn't operate in the name of a king or a church. These Asia-wide trading networks were based on kinship – forged by clans of Gujaratis or Jews or Armenians – but they operated in an environment in which money facilitated transactions among Hindus, Muslims and

Buddhists, of whatever nationality or tribe. Asian rulers didn't usually interfere in long-distance trade; port cities competed to attract commerce, which could be taxed. When states did try to control trade, as the Chinese would do in the latter part of this Asian Millennium, it usually ended in failure.

Buddhism was a vital sinew in this emerging network, particularly in East Asia. Islam would play the same role in Asia's west.

THE CHRISTIAN OUTLIER

Monotheism in the West goes back to Abraham, the father of Judaism, Christianity and Islam. Jewish views of wealth, while varying, have generally viewed poverty as an evil to be avoided. Along with a need for charity was a sense that people also had to look after themselves. Old Testament figures, from Abraham to Jacob and Solomon, were viewed as meriting their wealth.

As Jewish life shifted from the farm (and exile) to the Hellenic cities, rabbinical thought encompassed the need to look after others as well as one's capital. This would endure throughout Jewish commercial life, with family networks penetrating the known world. But Jews, everywhere a minority, lacked the state support to transform their attitudes into government policy.

Christianity's early years were similarly on society's fringe but would eventually find political power in the conversion of Emperor Constantine the Great. Christianity also had the same impact on human world views as Buddhism, opening minds to the idea of a linear history – a direction, a future, that would be different than the present. The Judeo-Christian heritage played the same supporting role as Buddhism for the development of credit. But Jews remained a minority, while Christianity's influence on money was far more convoluted. The New Testament repeatedly presents Jesus's views that poverty is holy and wealth is an impediment to salvation.

It's easier for a camel to pass through the eye of a needle than a rich man to enter heaven

In the Book of Matthew, Jesus tells a rich young man that, if he wants to get to heaven, he should sell his possessions and give everything to the poor. This message doesn't go down well. But in the Book of Luke (18:18-30), in a similar episode, Jesus goes further: "Jesus looked at him and said, 'How hard it is for the rich to enter the kingdom of heaven. Indeed, it is easier for a camel to go through the eye of a needle than for someone who is rich to enter the kingdom of heaven.'"

Temples in many faiths have served as quasi-banks or clearing houses. But not in Christianity's earliest centuries. The gospels tell the story of how Jesus chased the moneychangers out of the Temple of Jerusalem. Jesus acknowledged money as a fact of life, but one to be separated from faith. He told his fellow Jews to pay taxes to secular powers: "Render unto Caesar the things that are Caesar's, and unto God the things that are God's" (Matthew 22:21).

While these teachings laid the groundwork for modern ideas of separating church and state, they also denounced elevating wealth above Christian values such as love and charity. Although a fair interpretation suggests Jesus wasn't against wealth per se, the early Church took a fundamentalist line that frowned on making money.

Christianity's future was assured when the eastern Roman emperor Constantine converted to the religion. His conversion freed him to raid pagan temples for their gold, suggesting his motivation was not entirely pure, but the religion stuck, and all future emperors remained Christian. The radical faith spread throughout the Byzantine and Italian worlds, hurried along by trade routes and market centres first laid down by the ancient Greeks.

Indeed, Christianity, like Buddhism, was an urban religion, revolutionary in its emphasis on individual salvation and its opposition to fertility or weather gods. Also, like Buddhism, it was universal rather than based on a sect, language or place. It especially appealed to the poor, the meek whom Jesus said would inherit the earth. But it was the commercial ties of the eastern Mediterranean – the bonds of money – that facilitated the adoption of this new common religion.

But in the western part of Europe, Christianity applied the brakes to the return of money in the post-Roman world, reinforcing Dark Age feudalism. Byzantium endured, but its monetary affairs remained based on the strength of its gold solidus (known there as the bezant) and a preference for coins over credit. It would take something new to shake up this world of stagnant money.

ISLAM AND EARLY CAPITALISM

Islam exploded onto the scene from seventh-century Arabia, a harsh land of idolatry on the fringes of world intercourse. Muhammad, a merchant, received the message of God in Mecca, a trading centre. In 622, he fled with his followers to Medina and founded the Muslim community.

From there they embarked on a stunning act of conquest. Islam emerged from under the shadow of two great empires, Byzantium and Sasanian Iran. Within 100 years, the new faith had brought Arabia, Egypt, Iran, Iraq and Syria under its sway. Then it conquered its way into northern India to the east and Spain to the west.

Unlike Judaism or Christianity, Islam from the very start combined religion and secular power. Its early kingdoms were ruled by caliphs, whose authority came from being of the line of Muhammad's appointed successors or, in the case of Shiism, his son-in-law Ali.

Before becoming the Prophet of God, Muhammad had been a businessman, as were some of his companions. The Koran had plenty of warnings concerning greed, but it did not condemn wealth or commerce. On the contrary, the Koran encouraged wealth so long as it was gained in a moral way and put to good purpose.

Hence one mandatory duty of a Muslim is to give alms – the *zakat* – thereby ensuring the rich help the poor. But even more influential in the story of money is the Koran's prohibition against charging interest (*riba*). Koranic scripture is concerned with both salvation in the next world and social justice in this one.

But usury, and the debt it creates, has been necessary to every civilisation. Muslims quickly invented tools to sidestep the limits imposed by their faith – tools that would be later copied and industrialised by Europeans. Mesopotamia had developed banking in the absence of coinage. The Greeks had created a market economy based on coins which blunted the need for banking. And Rome had introduced fiat currency. The Muslims were the first to put together the full package for the sake of commercial finance.

Caliph Abd al-Malik issued the first Islamic coins from a longstanding Damascus mint in 696, or 77 years into the faith's history, including a gold dinar (modelled after the Byzantine solidus) and a silver dirham (the name derived from the Roman denarius).

To ensure the quality of coins, Islamic authorities cut off the hands of money forgers

Muslim unease with portraiture led to coins being printed with calligraphy proclaiming the unity and uniqueness of God and Muhammed as his prophet.

In 702 one of Malik's governors founded the first Islamic mint in Wasit, Iraq. To ensure the quality of coins, authorities promised to cut off the hands of minters or moneychangers caught counterfeiting. The Abbasid ruler al-Mamum introduced in 813 standards for coins that included his name. From here on, there were two ways Muslim rulers asserted their divine right: by having their name called during Friday prayers, and by having their name on coins.

Silver dirhams especially became accepted currency throughout even Christian Europe. They financed the Islamic Golden Age, a period of scientific, artistic and commercial fervour.

The greatest fortunes, however, went to those who controlled the money supply. The biggest providers of ingots for Arab coinage were gold-producing lands on the southern edge of the Sahara Desert, especially the kingdom of Mali. One of its kings, Mansa Musa, made a pilgrimage to Mecca in 1324. This was no ordinary hajj; Musa came to impress.

He stopped off in Cairo to show off his vast entourage, including 14,000 slave girls dedicated to his pleasure, and handed out vast sums to the mosques, in the souks and to local aristocrats. He spent so much money, estimated to be as much as 18 pounds of pure gold, that he depressed the price of precious metals for years. In the end, he gave away everything and had to get a loan in Mecca to finance his journey home. But Musa had certainly made an impression: flaunting African gold put it on maps everywhere, like a great X marking the spot.

Coins underwrote the caravans and ships connecting Cordoba to Cairo, Mali to Malaysia. Arab and Persian businessmen, including world-spanning family conglo-merates called *karimis*, travelled far and wide. But coins were secondary to their financial arrangements. The Muslim traders spread credit, into India, into Russia and into Italy.

From the very beginnings of Islamic history, traders in Mecca found ways around the prohibition of usury by basically hiding it in transactions. This was the birth of "financial engineering" or "structured products", to use the modern parlance. For example, a creditor would bury the interest in a separate agreement.

To circumvent problems caused by uncertain coins or the hazards of not being paid from long-distance trade, Muslim bankers came up with the bill of exchange or letter of credit, called the suftajah.

Unlike previous banking tools such as promissory notes (which had existed for millennia and involved a merchant promising to pay later for what they wanted today), bills of exchange were written by the creditor and relied on third parties to facilitate payments. This made them more secure, but also allowed them to use tricks to avoid religious censure. Payments could be delayed or credit could be charged at a higher rate than was received in cash (to hide interest).

Alongside bills of exchange, Muslim traders also developed the *sakk* (a cheque, an immediate claim to payment from a bank). Private merchants pooled their capital, and their risk, in partnerships called *mudarabah*, in which profits and losses were shared equally.

Many of these practices predated Islam but took off after two developments starting in the eighth century.

First, the Arabs adopted the use of numerals, copied from India. For the first time, capitalism was expressed in a decimal system using zero. This allowed banking instruments to flourish and to be calculated anywhere in the world. It also led to requirements for bankers to keep records and ledgers of all transactions. Double-entry book-keeping, using "Arabic" numerals, paved the way for the widespread use of bills of exchange. It allowed for the rise of merchant houses that could track not just individual transactions, but the entire circulation of capital flowing in and out of their far-flung posts.

Second, with the help of Jewish translators, caliphs such as Mamum, with his "House of Wisdom" in Baghdad, began copying the works of classical Greece. They also drew on Indian, Persian and Chinese ideas, but especially Greek philosophy, medicine, science and literature. Among these were concepts such as *oikos*, the management of the estate, which helped inform the great Muslim trading houses.

Mercantile groups such as the Arab *karimi*, as well as Jewish, Armenian and other ethnic family operations, were private traders who also financed state projects. Unlike previous aristocrats, they were not landowners or tax collectors. They were capitalists. They established *funduqs*, large commercial institutions and markets that combined warehouses, stock exchanges and futures markets. Every major city came to have one, including Samarkand, Baghdad, Basra and Cairo. And with the Buddhist routes along the Silk Road, they helped weave Asia into a super-connected world of commerce with money as its bloodstream.

There were limits, however, to what could be achieved in the Islamic world. Islamic strictures still counted for something, limiting financial tools to major trading houses but not governments or everyday life. Businesses had to balance wealth with social considerations. Many of these lands were arid, and therefore resource-constrained, putting natural limits on economic growth. The Golden Age of Islam came to a brutal end in the 13th century with the Mongol sack of Baghdad.

The Mongols brought with them not just death and destruction. They had a surprise for the Muslim world: a new kind of currency, one that was hard to believe as real. It would completely upend the meaning of faith.

WOMEN ON COINS

Female portraits show up frequently on coins and banknotes, and sometimes their symbols are no different than those of men's. The ancient Greeks used imagery of their cities and striking patron goddesses such as Demeter, Athena and Aphrodite. It was Alexander the Great who began splashing his own face across the known world, an excess avoided by the stern Roman Republic.

But as Rome transformed into an empire, coinage became a principal form of propaganda. **FULVIA FLACCA BAMBULA**, born around 83BCE, married three politicians and, in the wake of Julius Caesar's assassination, found herself in charge of Italy. As Octavian, Pompey and her final husband Mark Antony duked it out in the Eastern Mediterranean, she commanded the Roman mint in Lugdunum (today Lyon, France) to strike a silver coin that depicted the goddess of Victory in her own likeness.

Fulvia lost her bid for power to Octavian, but soon other influential women put their faces on coins, most famously **CLEOPATRA** – another lover of Mark Antony and victim of Octavian. The Byzantine empire also featured powerful women on coins, but its female iconography was more commonly religious, such as portrayals of Mary, mother of Jesus.

As coinage circulated once more in Europe after the Dark Ages, women rulers were rare, and rarely portrayed on coins. A medieval pope, John, might have actually been a Joan, a legend supported by the existence of **POPE JOAN** silver coins from the ninth century. More often, though, when queens commissioned coins, they followed Fulvia's example, essentially copying masculine iconography to assert their right to rule.

For example, **URRACA LÉON-CASTILLA** ruled Spain from 1109 to 1126 and was the first Iberian woman to issue coinage. She did so following the example of her father, printing her name as a Rex rather than a Regina. Her contemporary, **MATILDA**, daughter of Henry I of England, struck coins that proclaimed her gender-neutral "IMP" instead of using her title as imperatrix. Another contemporary, **DUCHESS BERTHA OF LORRAINE**, presented herself on horseback, brandishing a sword and riding astride – like a man.

06
PAPER

The Mongols confiscated metallic money, forcing people to use paper substitutes

Money is not just FinTech, or financial technology. It's "culture-tech" too. When a society rapidly introduces a new monetary technology, it can create jarring differences in how people conduct themselves. For people in such a place, the change is profound, but usually incremental. It's only when people from outside experience the new regime that the degree of change becomes obvious.

Take, for example, now: 2019. Over the past decade, China's leading internet companies, Alibaba and Tencent, have transformed their online businesses, for shopping and for games, respectively, into all-encompassing worlds built around payments.

Today, Tencent's messaging app, WeChat, lets users do more than just send messages and play games. By introducing proto-money in the form of *lai see* (red-packet money), WeChat became a giant payments network. Giving cash in red packets is a longstanding tradition in Chinese society, and Tencent, the company that owns WeChat, digitised the process. From there it added all kinds of services, from ordering food to investing in stocks.

Similarly, Alibaba took its e-commerce site and set up payment connections among businesses and consumers. Then it allowed people to put shopping money held in escrow into the equivalent of a money-market fund, which provided better returns than the interest in a bank deposit. China's traditional banking sector was notorious for poor service, so Alibaba's fund caught on like wildfire once people decided it was trustworthy.

The upshot of these "super apps" is that almost all aspects of daily life in China, from catching a cab to visiting a restaurant, are done through either the Alibaba or Tencent network – to the extent that foreign visitors find they can no longer use their overseas credit card or even local cash. China has moved so rapidly into digital finance that it has literally left the rest of the world behind.

This is not the first time foreign visitors have felt this dissonance when arriving in China. Nor is the super app the first financial innovation to set China apart. To understand China's first great financial innovation – paper money – we must return to the peak of the Arab Golden Age and the Islamic and Buddhist connections that fused Asia into a giant trading zone.

One of the most celebrated merchant riders of the Muslim trading rails was Mohammed Ibn-Battuta. Born in Tangiers, he made the hajj to Mecca in 1325 and just kept going, leading a life of adventure on the road that he later recorded. In 1346, at the behest of the Sultan of Delhi, he journeyed to Quanzhou (or Zaiton, as he called it), a port city on the Chinese coast in Fujian province.

From the 11th through 14th centuries, Quanzhou served as China's principal port for foreign traders. It was a giant, cosmopolitan city with Buddhist, Muslim, Christian and Hindu communities, each with their own networks extending throughout China.

China at this time was under Mongolian control, following a series of invasions that began with Genghis Khan and was completed by his grandson Kublai Khan. But although Kublai had conquered China, the Mongols gradually submitted to the supremacy of Chinese culture.

In 1271, Kublai declared he had the "mandate of heaven" to launch a Chinese dynasty, the Yuan. He did things expected of a Chinese emperor, such as supporting schools for Confucian scholars, leading courtly rituals to protect agriculture and commerce – and issuing paper money.

Seventy years later, paper money would still have the power to astonish foreign visitors, even seasoned travellers such as Ibn-Battuta. He wrote:

The people of China do not do business for dinars and dirhams...they buy and sell with pieces of paper the size of the palm of the hand, which are stamped with the Sultan's stamp. Twenty-five

Much like tourists without an Alibaba app in China today, people could no longer pay with coins

such pieces are called balisht [cash], which is the same as dinar among us....If anyone goes to the bazaar with a silver dirham or a dinar intending to buy something with it, it is not accepted and he is disregarded until he pays with [cash].

In this regard, Ibn-Battuta was not alone, nor the first. Marco Polo journeyed through Asia from 1271 to 1295, in the earliest years of the Yuan dynasty. Whereas Ibn-Battuta was on a private voyage and never rubbed shoulders with the khans, Polo became a trusted advisor and functionary to Kublai, serving at his capital in Khanbalik, as Beijing was then called. But Marco Polo was also greatly impressed by paper money. He wrote: "With regard to the money of Khanbalik, the great khan may be called the perfect alchemist, for he makes it himself."

Polo described how the Chinese manufactured notes from the bark of the mulberry tree, the leaves of which provide food for silkworms. Paper money, or "cards", as Polo called them, were valued up to "ten bezants", as he wrote in his Travels: "All these cards are stamped with [the khan's] seal, and so many are fabricated that they would buy all the treasuries in the world. He makes all his payments in them, and circulates them throughout his kingdoms and provinces over which he holds dominion; and none dares to refuse them under pain of death."

To ensure his paper money was accepted, the khan also confiscated all gold and silver coins. Foreign merchants such as Marco Polo and Ibn-Battuta were required to hand over their bullion for paper notes, at rates determined by a panel of Chinese moneychangers. This bullion was held on deposit until they wished to leave the country. Their inability to use their metal coins is like the modern visitor who finds she can't get by without an Alibaba or Tencent app. Ibn-Battuta remarked on the surveillance state in China, which required him to constantly update local police on his movements. However, he also noted how safe it was to travel throughout the country–observations that sound like China today.

To ensure paper money was accepted, Kublai Khan forced merchants to hand over their bullion

Of course, the more onerous the rules, the more valuable the rewards of skirting them. Ibn-Battuta related how some merchants sidestepped this by melting down coins into ingots and hiding them in the lodges of foreign communities. He had arrived at Quanzhou at the peak of the paper-money system, and already people were chafing at the government's restrictions. This again echoes today's China, in which wealthy people go to great lengths to send their money overseas by evading Beijing's control of the export of capital.

But in Polo's time, nearly a century before Ibn-Battuta described attempts at cheating the system, the khan's paper money held sway. The threat of execution was taken seriously. "This is the reason why the khan has more treasury than any other lord in the world," Polo noted.

Paper money was a revolutionary step in the history of money because it came to represent the first true example of fiat money, or money that existed purely because of government decree, without any intrinsic value. Even in the excesses of third-century Rome, silver coins still contained some actual silver, but paper was worth zero without faith in the government behind it.

Both Polo and Ibn-Battuta recognised that only a very powerful state, controlling an effective bureaucracy and a fearsome justice system, could issue paper money and get people to accept it. The khan's threat about pain of death was real, and everyone in his realm knew it. It would take Europe almost 400 years after Ibn-Battuta's journey to experiment with paper money.

MONEY IN CHINA
Indeed, whether as pioneer or laggard, China had been a currency outlier for most of its history. Only the importation of Buddhism made any deep impact on this civilisation, which otherwise developed a huge, technologically sophisticated economy in isolation from the rest of the world.

China was probably the first place to produce coins, in the form of cowry shells cast in bronze or copper. Ancient dynasties produced coins in the shape of agricultural implements such as spades and knives, probably for gifts and tributes before they became methods of payment.

Chinese culture recognised the metaphorical nature of money early on. The Book of Master Guan, compiled in 26BCE but attributed to 645BCE, said, "You cannot wear money, but you can be warm; you cannot eat money, but you can fill your belly."

In 221BCE, the Qin emperor – the first to unite northern China – homogenised the realm's currency around a standard coin, the *ban liang* (half ounce), forms of which had been around for about 200 years. It was notable for its round shape with a square hole. Later in the Han dynasty, experiments with the coin's weight settled on a "five-grain" (of rice) standard, in which form the *ban liang* would endure as China's primary currency until the late 19th century. (Europeans would call these coins "cash", from the Sanskrit term for bronze coins, *karshapana*, a word that had entered China in tandem with Buddhism.)

Coins were so prevalent and enduring in China that they became a marker of Chinese culture, along with things such as calligraphy or porcelain. Neighbouring countries adopted many features of this culture, and Chinese coins served as the main form of money in Japan for centuries. But China failed to exploit coinage the way the Greeks and Romans had. With limited supplies of gold or silver, which circulated in China as ingots, coins continued to be made from low-value metals such as copper or its alloy, bronze. China would not mint its first silver coin until 1890. This suited the emperors just fine because another enduring hallmark of Chinese civilisation has been insistence by its governments on controlling commerce.

That difference of approach is manifest in the coins themselves. Ancient Chinese belief held that the earth was square and the heaven a dome, and the mandate of heaven gave the emperor the power to serve as the conduit between the two. Therefore, the *ban liang*, as the symbol of the emperor, was shaped to represent this symbiosis. The coin was later also seen to represent the Daoist ideas of yin and yang.

The *ban liang* was designed to be practical as well. Chinese mints forged these on square rods, creating the central holes, which were then used to string together coins in groups of a hundred or a thousand.

But lugging around strings of low-value bronze coins was not suitable for large-scale commerce. Instead, macro-sized industry was reserved for the state, and coins were relegated to small, daily transactions. Merchants, similarly, were relegated to the lower rungs of society, and ancient philosophers took a dim view of money. Yang Hu, a contemporary of Confucius, wrote, "He who seeks to be rich, will not be benevolent. He who wishes to be benevolent, will not be rich." It's a sentiment that Plato, who lived a century later, would have applauded.

So long as economic growth was limited and alternatives existed to bronze coins (such as silk cloth, which was also used for payments), the cumbersome use of coins was manageable. But the emergence of Buddhist pilgrimage trails, combined with Sui and Tang dynasty encouragement of Silk Road trade, took China on an unexpected journey.

FINANCING GROWTH

By the fall of the western Roman Empire, India had become the centre of the world's economic gravity. But that honour then shifted to China. By the eighth century, the Tang dynasty oversaw the world's biggest economy with a capable bureaucracy. It built on technological innovations such as paper and printing, gunpowder and porcelain. It also augmented earlier triumphs, such as by using the Grand Canal built during the preceding dynasties to connect the dry north to the Yangtze River delta.

During the Tang dynasty, China began a shift of population and activity from the northern Yellow River delta south to the surrounding areas of the Yangtze River. Until then the vastness of China had been largely unpopulated aside from small, scattered communities. That began to change as the growing population filled in the empty spaces, leading to diverse crops, new technologies and the development of river ports to manage trade.

This migration was internal and went unnoticed by the rest of the world, but it represented a claim to new lands and resources similar to those Europeans would gain from the New World. The Chinese, in other words, colonised China.

From the year 500 to 1000, China's population grew from 50m to 75m, the economy doubled in size and living standards reached unprecedented heights. Parts of the Islamic world experienced faster growth, but never at the scale of China.

This economic expansion could not be financed by stringing together low-value bronze coins. The Tang dynasty was a great importer of ideas, however, and along with Buddhism came the monasteries' commercial bent.

From India, by way of Buddhism, China acquired concepts such as compound interest, equitable mortgages, securities trading and venture capital. Moreover, Buddhism provided Tang China with the beginnings of a consumer culture because it required building monasteries, temples and rest houses; commissioning statuary and other forms of art; and financing festivals and pilgrimages.

Consumerism quickly inspired secular life. By the eighth century, the Tang court at Chang'an (Xian) had pioneered fashion and conspicuous taste in food, art, literature and appearance, long before Paris would make its mark. Wealth also went hand in hand with technological innovation: in this period, China invented gunpowder, the magnetic compass and printing (necessary to administering the exams to become a mandarin – and, later, to paper money). China, always present but peripheral, had become central to the world.

Earlier dynasties had permitted private merchants to strike coins so long as they met the local ruler's standards for weight and made their liquidity available to the state. The Qin in the second century BCE had taken control of minting. After that, dynasts would oscillate between allowing private mints and directly controlling the money supply. Coins were widespread but used mainly as a unit of account. The difficulty in using coins for bulk or long-distance trade led merchants to use promissory notes and bills of exchange. But, as the economy grew, governments became more dependent on money, and in the heady era of the Tang and into the Song dynasty (960-1276), their need grew acute.

PAPER MONEY
Now known as Chengdu, the city of Yizhou in Sichuan province had become a major commercial centre during the Tang dynasty. It combined a major printing industry with a guild of metalsmiths, which provided remittances to the government. But Sichuan was also big and remote, a realm unto itself, which gave it some latitude. A copper shortage in the last years of the Tang dynasty led local merchants to issue promissory notes on paper, exchangeable into bronze coins. These soon circulated as currency. Overprinting, abuse and liquidity problems led the local ruler to take control of paper issuance, with fixed denominations and two-year lifespans.

The experiment was a success, although it would take time for news of this to reach the emperor. Private merchants began issuing their own "flying cash", using it as travellers' cheques so they could deposit cash in one city and withdraw it in another, thereby avoiding the need to transport coins. The Tang dynasty, now late in its reign, tried to control these private markets by printing its own version of this paper. They didn't understand what they were doing, though. When people actually tried to redeem these notes for cash, the Tang government refused and the entire market collapsed.

The Tang dynasty soon disintegrated, and after a bloody interregnum, a new set of warlords established the Song dynasty. The economy was still expanding but the new government was beset by waves of invading horsemen tribes from the north. Coinage was being sucked into military budgets, so the Song emperors repeated the Sichuan experiment with paper money, issuing promissory notes to pay suppliers to the military that were redeemable at the Song capital, Kaifeng.

This capital was overrun by a kingdom of northern horsemen called the Jurgen, and the Song dynasty repositioned itself in the south. This disruption only encouraged its experiments in paper money, however. In Sichuan, the local government experimented with a new kind of paper money, the *qianyin*, that it required to be used for paying taxes and for military expenditures. This note was not redeemable in hard currency, making it the first true fiat money.

In 1161, the Song took this concept nationwide with a paper note called the *huizi*. It was theoretically exchangeable, with denominations ranging from 200 to 3,000 bronze coins. But doing so proved difficult, possibly because merchants didn't trust them, preferring hard currency (which they could also sell at a premium to coin-starved Japan, which used Chinese money). Pretty soon, no one could actually redeem *huizi* for coins. Bad money drove out the good.

Recognising the problem, the Song government declared *huizi* paper could not be exchanged for coins, and insisted it be used to meet tax obligations or to receive government payments. This is what made it the first national fiat currency.

The Portuguese dumped a vast supply of cowries on the market, causing bankruptcies throughout Asia

For a while, it worked, with merchants circulating paper money at close to its nominal value. Paper had its advantages. It was easy to transport and the government opened offices throughout the country where people could exchange damaged notes for fresh ones. It meant that the government was no longer dependent on random supplies of metal in the ground to finance its needs. The rulers felt as though they had finally achieved control of the supply of money.

The absence of coins led people to use other forms of commodity money, such as silk and cowry shells. Shells couldn't be counterfeited, but they too had their dangers. In the 16th century, the Portuguese, having established forts throughout the Indian Ocean, realised the centrality of cowries in the local economies. So they collected a vast supply of shells from the Maldives and dumped them on the market – a shock that instantly undermined their value and caused bankruptcies to ripple throughout Asia.

China proved immune to such nasty surprises because it controlled the supply of money. The Chinese experiment with fiat money set the precedent for today's world, in which the US dollar, the euro and other currencies derive their value from the authority of the state, not from any intrinsic worth. And from the 1160s to the 1190s, the experiment was a success.

But within this triumph lay its undoing: the government controlled the supply of money. At first paper, whether issued privately or by the state, was meant as a substitute for bullion. But issuers always wanted to print more than they could physically back.

LOSING CONTROL
The end of the Song dynasty during the 1200s was marked by military defeats and civil wars. As the Song emperors printed more paper notes to finance their military needs, these lost their value, but hoarding of

coins and bullion meant only paper was in circulation. Had China's geopolitical fortunes been better, it's possible the experiment in fiat currency would have proved durable. Instead, Chinese society began to suffer inflation, a strange experience that no one understood but could feel chipping away at living standards.

The Song fell to the Mongols in the 13th century before their experiment with paper money got out of hand. But Kublai Khan, after installing himself as the emperor of the new Yuan dynasty, began issuing his own paper money.

The Mongols had created the world's largest empire ever in a bout of energetic conquering reminiscent of the seventh-century Arab explosion, but bigger. This empire stretched from the Pacific Ocean through Central Asia and across the Arab world, northern India, and into Russia and the edges of Europe. As the Arabs had done, and Alexander the Great before them, the Mongols transformed their domains into a great free-trade zone, the better to tax it.

Doing so with strings of bronze coins wasn't going to cut it, so the Yuan rulers relied on printing paper. To ensure paper's success, the government had to do more than just pay their armies and bureaucrats with it, as Alexander the Great had done with coins. The Mongols confiscated metallic money wherever they could, forcing merchants and individuals to use paper substitutes. Foreign traders such as Marco Polo and Mohammed Ibn-Battuta had to hand over their silver and gold, to be held on deposit by bureaucrats.

In 1287, the Mongols issued a new paper note called the *zhiyuan chao*, which was the first not even nominally linked to silver or any other metal. Its value was based on the mightiness of Kublai Khan.

For a while it worked. Both Polo and Ibn-Battuta were astonished by the idea of paper money and the fact that no one in local markets would accept their foreign coins.

By the 1350s, though, as Ibn-Battuta was headed back to Morocco, the Chinese experiment with paper money had collapsed. The emperors had printed far too much, triggering rampant inflation. The empire was in disarray, and the loss of financial stability encouraged ethnic Chinese rebels to kick out their Mongolian overlords, establishing the Ming dynasty.

At first the Ming shared their predecessors' world-spanning ambitions. They sponsored the great Treasure Ship fleets under Admiral Zheng He. His epic voyages from 1405 to 1425 demonstrated Chinese naval prowess and cultural greatness from Java to East Africa. Having found no civilisation worthy of its own, but facing yet more bouts of pesky northern raids, the Ming dynasty retrenched. Trade would only be accepted in the guise of tribute, so that foreign merchants could be kept out. Later, to enforce this decree, the emperor ordered entire populations to evacuate the southern coastline, lest people trade with pirates.

By deliberately turning its back on the rest of the world, Chinese society gradually lost its curiosity, and therefore its culture of innovation. Little by little, dynamism leaked from East to West.

The policy of closing down foreign trade reflected a typical desire to control markets, but gradually the Ming faced even greater money problems. At first they were careful with paper issuance, having experienced how it had been abused. Subsequent emperors, however, couldn't resist the temptation. They turned on the printing presses. Beset by brazen ocean pirates and a new generation of northern horsemen raiders, the Ming faced a dire need for silver to finance their armies. By the early 16th century, the Ming had lost control of their currency and China was suffering from the first known case of hyperinflation.

Things were so bad that in 1567 the emperor grudgingly allowed private foreign trade at China's borders. In the South China Sea, Chinese merchants quickly struck up trade with "pirates" from nearby islands.

In 1570, a pair of Chinese junks sailed into Manila harbour. The Chinese from nearby Fujian province had recently begun bartering with the island Malays for their gold dust and beeswax. This time the Chinese were shocked to encounter a pair of boats containing about 100 tough-looking Europeans.

They were even more surprised to learn these Europeans were just an expedition from a larger settlement further down the island chain, and that this community was being supplied from the east, across the Pacific Ocean. The Chinese didn't understand how this could be possible, as nothing existed in that direction other than Japan.

But whatever doubts the junks' captains had, they put them aside once they realised what the European vessels contained – silver. Lots of silver. The barbarians had materialised in China's backyard bringing ships full of money.

By the early 16th century, China was suffering from the first known case of hyperinflation

07

DISCOVERY

Hoping to find a new route to India, Columbus inadvertently stumbled across America

An Indian

There were many reasons for Europe's emergence from the Dark Ages. This journey of European exploration involved science, art, philosophy and other realms, but nothing represented it better than the ships sailing from Portugal and Spain in search of riches and glory.

The climax of the Age of Discovery, as the Europeans would call it, was Spain's creation of the first global trade route. It was also the last hurrah of empires built on coinage. Spain's failures with money would contribute to its demise, and the future of world power would be increasingly based on credit.

Spain and Portugal were the initial competitors in the race to find direct access to the riches of Asia, especially China. They were desperate to find a way around the hostile Muslim powers that had come to block their way, abetted by the shifty Italian city-states that enjoyed a monopoly on trade with the infidels.

Portugal won initial success, having begun staking positions along the western coast of Africa from the mid-15th century, in search of the goldmines that had made Mansa Musa so rich. Vasco da Gama led the first European voyage to reach India by sea, landing on the Malabar Coast in 1498. He did so by going around the African continent and inserting the Portuguese blade into the heart of Indian Ocean trade networks.

Spain's monarchs took a flyer on the "world is round" speculations of a wily Genovese seafarer known to them as Cristóbal Colón. They would reach China another way. Although Christopher Columbus persisted in the belief that his famous voyage of 1492 had reached Asia, it soon became clear that Spain had discovered a new world, one populated by great civilisations bedecked in gold.

The discovery of the New World triggered a rapid, unprecedented exchange in ecology. Plants, viruses, insects, animals and people intermixed. Along with changing diets and cultures, this so-called "Columbian Exchange" led almost overnight to new fortunes – in gold, slaves, sugar and tobacco. It also led to new depths of human misery, with the biological near-elimination of native Americans and the enslavement of indigenous people and then Africans to work mines and plantations.

Just as Columbus triggered the globalisation of ecology, the Spanish established the globalisation of economics. In 1565, a Spanish fleet sailed from Acapulco, Mexico, across the Pacific Ocean. Its captain, Miguel López de Legazpi, was charged with establishing a Spanish colony in the Philippines (known to Spain from the previous circumnavigation of Ferdinand Magellan, who had been killed there). Spain's King Philip II had given different instructions to the ship's navigator, a friar named Andrés de Urdaneta: to find the route back across the Pacific.

There had already been attempts to find the return route. Due to a political accommodation with Portugal, Spain was barred from making settlements eastward through the Indian Ocean. To directly access China, it needed to complete the Pacific passage. Urdaneta figured out that the currents leading back to the Americas were far to the north. Almost five months later, he achieved the *tornaviaje*, the return trip to Acapulco. Two-way shipping, the galleon trade, began in haste. Urdaneta had created the first maritime links connecting Europe, the Americas, Africa and Asia.

Chinese silk and porcelain, Indian cotton, and Asian tea and spices were shipped to Mexico and then to Europe, first as raw materials and later as finished products. Cutting out the Muslim and Italian middlemen made Asian products affordable to far more consumers. New Spain filled with Chinese, Filipinos, Europeans and Africans; Mexico City became the first city in the world comprised of people from all four continents. China's population swelled on the back of unfamiliar agricultural foods from the New World that could be grown in marginal lands, such as maize and sweet potatoes.

In the race to nab Asia's riches, Spain and Portugal had to evade hostile Muslim powers

The early conquistadors coveted the Aztecs' and Incas' gold. The Americans did not understand the Spaniards' desire for metal to be used as money. The Incas were cashless, while the Aztecs relied on commodity money in the form of cacao beans to facilitate trade.

The conquistadors stunned the natives with their ferocity, their weapons and their lust for gold. However, another weapon would be the true undoing of the American empires, one that the Spanish didn't even realise they possessed: invisible germs that had long circulated in the Eurasian continent, against which the isolated peoples of the Americas had no immunity. By the time Pizarro showed up in Peru, or Cortez in Mexico, disease had already decimated native populations.

Spanish greed for gold fuelled the conquest of the Americas, but it was silver that became the lifeblood of the first global networks. Pizarro had completed his conquest of the Incan capital by 1541 and sent the first hauls of American gold back to Spain. But in 1545 he discovered the Cerro Rico in modern-day Bolivia: the "rich hill", which contained the world's biggest deposit of silver ore. It was literally a mountain made of silver. The mining village there, Potosí, instantly became a boomtown.

Although Madrid insisted all New World treasure be shipped back to finance its myriad wars, the Spaniards in Mexico, with their new colony across the Pacific Ocean, quickly realised the Chinese would pay double or treble the rates for silver.

The Chinese possessed the manufactures that Europeans craved, but had little interest in European wares. On the other hand, money-starved China couldn't get enough of silver. Indeed, long before the British fostered a Chinese addiction to opium, the Chinese were hooked on Spanish silver, and the piece of eight, or *peso de ocho reales* (so called because one peso was worth eight official reales), became the global coin of trade.

This dependence would ultimately be China's undoing. When Urdaneta forged the final link in global trade, China was the world's biggest economy and most powerful country. Cities such as Beijing and Hangzhou, along with Cairo, Istanbul and Vijayanagara (south India) were populous and wealthy. Over the coming centuries, wealth and power would shift to Europe and its offspring in North America.

MONEY'S RETURN TO EUROPE

Europe's rise is often attributed to its exploitation of the resources of the New World. Its domination there arose from its fragmented, competitive, violent nations, which competed to acquire the tools of navigation and warfare needed to triumph. China, meanwhile, satisfied with the triumphs of its long civilisation, grew complacent and lost its innovative edge.

Missing from this narrative is the role of money. It wasn't that the Iberians lusted for gold and were sufficiently bold to get it, or that the Chinese had grown indifferent to foreign trade. It was the way money catalysed the Age of Discovery, made globalisation possible and then propelled Western dominance.

To understand this, we must take a step back and look at what was happening in medieval Europe. The fall of the western Roman Empire plunged Europe into a dark age marked by the decline of money in daily life and the hoarding of bullion, Christian bans on usury, the end of urban commerce in favour of manorial feudalism, and the loss of civic institutions.

The story of money – and therefore of civilisation's advance – shifted to the Asian world, linked across societies by Islam, Buddhism, common court etiquette and Silk Road caravans. The Islamic world developed tools such as bills of exchange to get around restrictions on charging interest on loans, and the Chinese invented paper money. Europeans would eventually discover these technologies and combine them in novel, far more effective ways.

The barbarian kingdoms that replaced Rome struck gold coins, mimicking Roman designs. Bishops in France began minting their own as well. But these were gold coins of high value, meant to bolster treasure hordes, and bullion was scarce. Small-value coins – pennies and the French sou – crept back into circulation around medieval fairs and were used for almsgiving. Arab silver dirhams also made their way into northern Europe via the Vikings, who sold European slaves down the Volga River to the Byzantine and Islamic worlds.

But for the most part coins were slow to return to people's daily lives, even when kings tried to circulate them. Charlemagne, who united much of western Europe from 774 to 812, was the first medieval king to mint coins bearing his image. His livre (from the Latin libra, for pound) was based on a pound of silver, and his standardisation provided western Europe with something similar to a unified currency.

But his empire didn't survive him and neither did his money. Charlemagne regarded money as primarily an expression of royal power. He tried to dictate prices and banned the Jews from lending money on the grounds that it offended Christian mores. Coinage throughout Europe remained limited to base metals modelled after the Roman denarius, such as the English penny.

The occasional discovery of new bullion sources sparked growth in the use of coins. Silver mines in Bohemia, for example, yielded new deposits in the 14th century. Nearby commercial towns such as Augsburg struck higher-value coins, and the local thaler (dollar) became a standard in Northern Europe.

But most transactions relied on barter. There were two impediments to remonetising Europe: the Church's strictures against usury, and the continued use of Roman numerals for counting.

Contact with the Muslim world changed this, first with the Crusades, then with the rise of Italian mercantile cities and finally with the Christian overthrow of Muslim Spain. Each of these led to financial renovations that made the Renaissance and the Age of Discovery possible.

THE CRUSADES AND THE TEMPLARS

Although the barbarian heirs to Rome tried to continue the Roman system of coinage, they could not control where the coins ended up. Money flowed to where there was real economic vitality: the urban centres of the Muslim world and beyond. And the lack of any standard or means of imposing purity on European coins left them open to constant debasement and shortages.

There were only two ways for Europeans to get their hands on valuable coins: export natural resources such as timber or slaves, or go to war and loot the Muslim worlds.

The Crusades were a Vatican-endorsed series of wars to liberate the Holy Land of Palestine from Muslim rule. Whatever their spiritual origins, the Crusades immediately devolved into plunder, both of Muslim lands and (Christian) Byzantium.

These wars, which took place during the 12th and 13th centuries, also created new financial demands. It was no easy thing to supply a long-distance military campaign, or to pay off suppliers, allies and ransoms.

Nor was it easy to move plunder safely back to Europe. European kings funded the Crusades through punitive taxation and forced loans, but the ships bearing soldiers returned carrying merchants who had bought Asian goods and now sought to offload them for a hefty profit. Whoever had coins in Europe spent these on Asian imports, so the bullion drain to the Muslim world only quickened.

The first quasi-banks in Europe emerged to address these problems, run not by merchants but by religious military orders such as the Knights Templar.

The Templars were founded in Jerusalem in 1118 to protect Christian pilgrims to the newly conquered Crusader states. They evolved into a professional fighting force with a string of fortifications across the Mediterranean. These castles soon doubled as vaults for confiscated treasure.

The Knights Templar became
financiers to French kings and the
papacy using bills of exchange

To facilitate the foreign exchange necessary to finance the Crusades and the trade that emerged in its wake, the Templars copied the Muslim inventions of bills of exchange and systems of accounting. Therefore, the knights could circumvent Vatican bans on interest while moving money safely on paper instead of dangerously by ship.

These tactics soon leaked to the wider world. The first known foreign-exchange contract in Europe was issued by a bank in Genoa in 1156 on behalf of two brothers. They borrowed 115 Genovese pounds to reimburse the bank's agents in Constantinople for 460 bezants (as the Byzantine solidus had become known). The payment in bezants was to take place one month after receiving the Genovese pounds. Nowhere was there a mention of the Genoan bank charging interest; instead it simply made sure the brothers paid its Byzantine representatives more than the amount borrowed.

Such techniques enabled the Templars to become Europe's go-to banking corporation, and their headquarters in Paris became a massive treasure house. Members, usually knights or other aristocrats, could deposit money or take out a loan in Paris but receive the funds as gold coins in Jerusalem – minus the Templars' fee.

Despite their vows of poverty, the Knights Templar became incredibly rich. Using bills of exchange and other Muslim financial tools, they became financiers to French kings and the papacy, even after the last of the Templars were kicked out of Palestine in 1291.

By then, however, the Templars had grown too rich and powerful for their own good. Philip IV of France took a dislike to an order that was operating beyond the control of the king, particularly one based in his own capital. He bullied the pope into abolishing the order in 1312, and then moved to confiscate its riches, burning the last Templar knights at the stake.

Philip IV opened his own royal treasury in the Louvre, setting the first example since the Roman Empire of a government asserting a monopoly over finances. But the Templars had introduced Europe to the basics of banking.

The next wave of contact with the Muslim world, via Italian city-states, would trigger a financial revolution.

FIBONACCI, THE MEDICIS AND ITALIAN BANKING

The Crusades had been good for Italian city-states such as Genoa and Venice, whose families built commercial networks throughout Turkey, Syria and Egypt to finance the rampaging armies. As their agents settled and assimilated in Byzantine and Ottoman communities, these Italian networks became intermediaries between the Christian, Jewish and Muslim worlds. They carefully observed the techniques that made Muslim traders so wealthy and imported these to Europe.

The most prominent such Italian, Leonardo of Pisa – better known as Fibonacci – was born around 1170 to a merchant family with a network in Algeria. Travelling there with his father, Leonardo was exposed to the Arabic-Hindu system of numerals and a decimal place.

Even then, six centuries after Rome's collapse, Europe continued to use Roman numerals. Roman numerals are a terrible way to count, let alone do mathematical calculations to determine, say, compound interest. The Romans, particularly after their republic became an empire, had relied on coins, not on banking. Their numerals reinforced this preference.

Incidentally, Chinese characters for counting were equally bad for calculations. Buddhists introduced Indian numerals in the eighth century, but the Chinese had already figured out decimal positioning on their own. Therefore, they didn't use numerals until the 19th century, preferring to rely on the abacus or on a more sophisticated but cumbersome technique of counting rods.

Fibonacci was not the first European to encounter Hindu-Arabic numerals, but he was the first to realise their commercial importance. He published his "Liber Abaci" ("Book of Calculation") in 1202. In it he showed how merchants could use this numbering system to calculate interest, handle fractions and quantify the notion of present value: how expectations of future revenues can be represented as a discounted value today.

It would take centuries for his arguments to be widely accepted in Europe. First, they flew in the face of orthodox beliefs about charging interest (and inertia around Roman numerals – never underestimate the power of rejecting innovation "because we've always done it this way"). Second, Fibonacci wrote in Latin at a time when books were rare, so his knowledge was confined to specialists. It was not until 1464, two and a half centuries later, that these ideas would be packaged as a businessman's bestseller. That was also the year Luca Paciolo, a friend of Leonardo da Vinci's and a tutor for the family of a Venetian banker, published a similar treatise. Paciolo's work was in vernacular Italian and came on the heels of the invention of the printing press, so it enjoyed wide distribution. Sometimes innovation takes a tortuous route.

For Italian city-states such as Venice, though, charging interest was fundamental to financing foreign trade. No merchant was going to put his money behind a ship or a voyage without expecting a big reward. Fibonacci gave them the tools to calculate the risks, the costs and just how big those rewards might be.

Christian families that engaged in the money business, like the Islamic merchants before them, relied on financial subterfuge to mask the true nature of their work. This use of jargon and complexities was baked into finance, and endures. But not everyone was handcuffed by neuroses about charging interest.

The Crusades had unleashed horrific, xenophobic violence against Jews throughout Europe. Jewish communities were banned from most fields of commerce. But their pragmatic views towards finance made them eligible for the dirty work of moneylending. Hence the Italian cities set up ghettos where the Jewish people could live and transact – and be controlled by Christian rulers, who quarantined them to the ghetto at night and on Christian holidays.

These early bankers, whether Jewish or Christians, were not much different from their predecessors dealing with coins in ancient Greece. They were moneylenders and loan sharks, forced to charge high interest because defaults were so likely, and quick to resort to violence when borrowers didn't pay up. The bankers got their name from their place of business: *banchi* (little benches), because they sat in the streets. It was hardly glamorous work.

Whereas the Templars had served solely the nobility, the earliest Italian *banchieri* served everyone. So long as a craftsman or merchant could pay, the bank would do business with them; only profits mattered. Gradually they became large enough to lend to aristocrats and kings – but these were bad clients, too ready to renege with impunity. Spectacular defaults like these sank many early banks, not least the emerging Medici family of 14th-century Florence.

The Medicis were foreign-exchange dealers who catered to the wealthy. They flourished by using bills of exchange to hide interest payments and by deploying Fibonacci's numerals and accounting tricks to keep track of everything in bound leather books.

They started out like other financiers, sitting on their benches outdoors, and like other financiers, they were ruined by royal defaulters – but the Medicis survived and transformed banking into a centre of power.

How? By diversifying. Banking, they realised, was about scale and breadth. If foreign exchange was volatile, the Medicis would rely on deposits and lending to drive other sources of revenue. If a prince was a potential defaulter, then bets had to be spread widely enough to ride out the occasional disaster. But the Medicis went one step further, diversifying out of banking and into city politics. By the early 15th century, the family patriarch, Giovanni di Bicci de' Medici, was generally acknowledged to be the real authority in Florence.

Bankers such as the Medicis formed guilds like the Arte de Cambio to distinguish them from the grubby moneylenders and pawnbrokers in the street. But their thirst for status never clouded their pragmatic attitude towards minorities. The Medicis had close ties to Florence's Jewish community, and in times of trouble, they used their wealth to protect them from Catholic zealots.

Most famously, however, Italian bankers used their awesome wealth to patronise the explosion of art, cuisine and architecture – all the better to fill their growing acquisitions of palaces and estates. What the accident of birth into an aristocracy could not give them, the bankers would buy: status. The Medicis underwrote the Renaissance in Florence, from Michelangelo to Leonardo da Vinci.

The Renaissance was about more than rich families funding artists and the city's greatest buildings and gardens. Money changed the way people thought and conducted themselves. Humanism infused Italian cities with new perspectives on art, architecture, science, politics and literature. For the elite, that translated into a cosmopolitan outlook. This cultural flowering was the vanguard of Europe's ascent. And it went hand in hand with Italian bankers' mastery of money.

The Italians adopted techniques from Islamic prototypes, which created effects across European society that were never allowed to happen in the Muslim (or Chinese) world. In Asia, money remained a tool for governments to wield. Family conglomerates and long-distance traders such as Mohammed Ibn-Battuta used financial tools in isolated, private transactions. In China, the elites were scholarly bureaucrats, and merchants were low-class types to be controlled, much like a necessary evil.

In Italy, the bankers became the government or joined the ruling oligarchy. The Italian city-states were constantly fighting one another, which required financing for mercenary armies. They did so by forcing the wealthiest merchants to loan money. Merchants were happy to do so because, as these were forced loans, the rulers decided the bans on usury didn't apply. This wasn't unusual in Europe – the same had been done in France and England to fund the Crusades. But in Florence, these loans could be sold. A merchant who needed cash found a ready market of other Florentine citizens who would accept his debt for a price, plus the right to collect the interest from the city government when the loan was due.

These forced loans became liquid assets, and bankers were confident they could call back the money from borrowers. Within the small world of wealthy Florence, families knew whom they could trust (and at what price). *Credere* (to believe) became the basis for credit. Huge sums could be lent by simply amending names and sums in a ledger. These innovations expanded commerce for everyone. Bills of exchange were created to work around usury laws, but they ended up expanding the supply of money. A loan appeared on a bank's ledger as an asset for the bank and a liability for the borrower, repayable at a later date. But that money was available immediately for the borrower to spend. For large merchants, a shortage of coins or gold and silver no longer prevented the movement of funds – nor held back their purchasing power

For banks, debt contracts with fixed terms required repayment regardless of what happened to the enterprise the loan was meant to fund. This made them valuable. The Italians invented tradable IOUs, what we call today the bond market.

Bankers in money centres such as Venice and Florence could exchange other currencies or gold and silver at the lowest, most stable rates. They used bills of exchange either to carry out transactions, or

The *banchieri* also lent to the aristocracy, who were all too ready to renege with impunity

as tradable instruments – money in their own right. Therefore, the Venetian ducat became the standard coin throughout the eastern Mediterranean, even in Muslim lands, while the Florentine florin proved to be the most popular currency in western Europe.

No longer did coins need to be shifted in bulk. Relatively small deposits with an Italian bank could be lent out to multiple borrowers at the same time, expanding the supply of money regardless of the number of coins in circulation.

This is called, in modern lingo, "fractional-reserve banking", which means the bank need keep only a fraction of its capital in its vaults to meet routine demands among depositors withdrawing their coins. The more deposits that can be redirected into loans, the more money the bank makes for itself and the more credit it creates in the economy. No longer was the supply of money tied to the amount of bullion. Instead the underlying base of gold or silver deposits could be reused multiple times – assuming the bankers kept enough on reserve to handle emergencies, and that the loans they extended were repaid.

Double-entry book-keeping and the use of cheques (a form of a bill of exchange, a written instruction to move money between accounts) added flexibility and security to the system. A thief could steal a shipment of coins, but stealing a bill of exchange proved worthless.

More significantly, this accumulation of credit and debts was entirely private – an affair between commercial bankers. Money was no longer just about minting or depositing coins, which meant bankers no longer had to rely on sovereign powers to create or circulate money. Banks were already familiar with hiding interest through bills of exchange, but now financial tools and ledgers became deliberately complex to keep rulers and taxmen in the dark about this new, private monetary system.

But bankers were still vulnerable to politics. The Medicis were brought down when Florence's fortunes fell amid a French invasion, and the family was expelled from the city in 1494. Their opulent wealth could not protect them from the resentment of the mob. A populist monk, Girolamo Savanarola, urged a peasant uprising to burn the Medicis' bank records in a "bonfire of the vanities".

RECONQUISTA

The tools created by Italian bankers came just in time for the influx of gold and silver from the New World. But even before the epic voyages of da Gama and Columbus, Europe was awakening to Muslim learning – in Spain and Portugal.

Arab and North African Berber armies conquered the Iberian Peninsula in 711, incorporating the former Visigoth kingdom into the Muslim world. Almost immediately, Christian rulers began chipping away at Muslim power in a long campaign known as the Reconquista. This effort was later sanctioned as a Crusade, attracting fighters from France and beyond. A series of invasions and civil wars ensued, culminating seven centuries later in total Christian control of the peninsula in 1491.

The Reconquista, then, took a long time. Little by little, Christians caught a glimpse of Muslim learning. As early as 967, a future pope, Sylvester II, journeyed to Barcelona to learn the Muslim secret of Arabic numerals. He failed to convince Europeans to abandon Roman numerals but introduced another Asian tool, the abacus, which allowed people to make speedy calculations without Arabic numerals (another example of technologies used by ancient Greece and Rome that Europe had forgotten).

By the mid-12th century, with Iberia fragmented among various Christian and Muslim kingdoms, European scholars began hunting among libraries in conquered cities such as Toledo for Muslim translations of ancient Greek texts. There, they discovered writings by authors such as Plato, Aristotle, Euclid and Galen that no one in the Christian world knew existed.

Christian Europe was rediscovering its own heritage via the great explorations, compilations and innovations of the Arab Golden Age. New vistas in mathematics, science, astronomy and medicine appeared. So did the prospect of riches from the East. This was the true Age of Discovery.

Spain was conquered in a cauldron of religious crusading, and the triumphant monarchs, Ferdinand of Aragon and Isabella of Castile – and their Christian rival, Alfonso V of Portugal – were bent on yet more war against Muslims. Columbus was in Spain when Granada, the final Muslim enclave, fell. The Portuguese were already fighting their way down the African coast. With the fall of Granada, Isabella was now the most powerful monarch in Europe, and she granted Columbus's request to lead an expedition across the Atlantic Ocean.

But even she was unwilling to finance such a speculative venture by herself. Besides, Isabella may not have had access to enough money; Spanish monarchs had already acquired a reputation for defaulting. Columbus financed about a quarter of the expedition costs himself – by getting a loan from a bank in Genoa.

The discovery of the New World was a watershed that initially made Spain incredibly wealthy. Gorging on Potosí silver, the Spanish crown financed one war after another, particularly ones to subdue Protestant rebels in its Netherland holdings. But something unexpected happened.

After an initial rush, Spain didn't get rich. It got poor. Spain had all the gold and silver, but the Italians and the Dutch grew wealthy and powerful.

How could this be possible? How could the spoils of conquest and the opening of trade with China lead to Spain's downfall?

Money wasn't what it used to be. It had transformed into something far more powerful.

08
CAPITALISM

By the end of the 16th century, Madrid went bankrupt, and the heady era of *largueza* turned into the gloomy *desengaño*

LARGUEZA

DESENGAÑO

New World silver flooded Europe and China, and the Spanish piece of eight became the first currency to be traded globally. Iberian monarchs believed that, as they now had more silver coins than anyone else, they were the richest, most powerful government. And for a time, that was true, and Spain embarked on a series of ruinous wars paid for by Potosí silver.

But Spain was just repeating the Roman Empire's example of basing its economy on plunder. There were productive industries in Spain: Burgos and Toledo were manufacturing towns for textiles. They boomed in the early period of the *largueza* (abundance) as bullion poured in. Yet by the end of the 16th century, Madrid went bankrupt and the heady era of *largueza* turned to that of the gloomy *desengaño* (disillusion), with industry undermined, wars lost and towns emptied.

Spain wasn't the only society minting coins at a rapid pace. Gutenberg's invention of moveable type in 1440 was soon adapted by Leonardo da Vinci to "print" coins en masse in standard formats. Rulers took to minting with gusto, assuming that wealth equated to more coins. For the first time since the Roman Empire, coins became part of people's daily lives, but at a much lower level of value.

Yet while all of Europe was engaged in the minting and debasement of coins, in Spain sudden wealth turned into unexpected poverty.

INFLATION AND FINANCIALISATION

Spain's elite believed money's value was static, based purely on the supply of precious metals. Therefore, she with the most silver won. Isabella and her fellow rulers failed to understand that bullion does not come with a preordained value. To be worth something, money must be wanted by someone else.

Spain flooded the world with silver, generating an initial uplift of wealth that boosted the Spanish economy,

but they delivered too much supply, too quickly. The European economy hadn't grown to the point where there was sufficient demand to meet all of this new silver. As such, metal coins lost their value, which is to say, prices of everything else rose. This is called inflation.

Just as Nero kicked off Rome's habit of debasing coins, the Spanish inadvertently did the same thing. Europe experienced the Price Revolution, a 100-year period beginning around 1540 in which the prices of food and other basic goods rose for the first time in centuries. By 1640, one piece of silver could only buy about 15% of what it could in 1540. (The impact of the Price Revolution in China was even more extreme.)

European society was conditioned to prices being static and this inflation came as a nasty surprise, particularly to the poor, who had to pay more for food. But it also led to new thinking about money and usury. Bypassing usury prohibitions was by now routine, with the Vatican itself happy to allow Italian bankers to bury fees in foreign-exchange contracts issued on the pope's behalf. But charging interest remained illegal everywhere.

The Price Revolution, however, challenged this stasis. too many borrowers were at risk of default as the value of their assets was inflated away. As the trading of bills of exchange spread from Italy to Augsburg, Amsterdam and London, governments began allowing more instances of exempting payment terms from usury laws.

And when governments were at risk of default, they also sought ways around usury laws. It's no coincidence that England's King Henry VIII, after breaking with the Catholic Church (with himself at the head of the new Church of England), was also the first monarch to legalise the payment of interest, in 1545.

At first, as far as Spain's rulers were concerned, the situation was fantastic. Through a combination of strategic alliances and conquests, Spain had come to rule over the Hapsburg Empire, whose remit included

The Spanish never understood that power was no longer about who owned the most coins

the Low Countries and the many successor states to the Holy Roman Empire. At its peak, Spain dominated both continental Europe and the New World.

Its finances came to be underwritten by the Fugger family of Augsburg. The Fuggers literally took over from the Medicis as Europe's preeminent merchant family, having seized the Medicis' assets when that family came to ruin in 1494. The Fuggers started as importers of Asian luxury goods, selling indulgences for the Church and outfitting the Hapsburgs with fine clothes. Under Jakob Fugger, the family really hit pay dirt when it extended loans to German noblemen who put up copper mines as collateral, which gave birth to the family's empire in mining and metals. Its silver operations made the local thaler the dominant currency throughout the Hapsburgs' German lands, from which the Spanish dollar got its name. Jakob Fugger completed his climb when he went from supplying the Hapsburgs with clothes to extending them loans. It was Fugger who put Italian banking methods to the service of Spain and financing its New World empire.

But while Spain's main banker understood money, its rulers did not. The crown taxed people in silver, based on weight, so inflation undercut the value of its income – the concept of indexing taxes to the value of silver

simply never occurred to anyone. The more coins Madrid possessed, the harder it was to finance its armies. The royals actually ended up borrowing again. Given the court's reputation for defaulting, bankers charged ever-higher rates of interest. To afford this, Madrid began mortgaging future shipments of treasure.

Spain might have shrugged off these setbacks had it put New World windfalls to productive ends and grown its domestic economy. Instead the royals spent their spoils on exotic Asian imports and on wars, as had the elites of the Roman Empire. By the 1640s, Spain was living far beyond its means. Depleted by war, the steep devaluation of silver and creditors' mistrust of the crown, Spain had lost its place as Europe's pre-eminent power to France and England.

The first dynamic in Spain's rise and fall was inflation caused by debasing the currency. The second dynamic at play was how the influx of money led to the financialisation of Spain's economy and society. Financialisation means the triumph of the financial sector and narrow money interests at the expense of other parts of society.

Merchants and landowners became addicted to easy money and stopped investing in productive activities. Instead they became the rentier class. Spanish aristocrats earned income from taxation, claims on New World properties and investment in bonds issued by the government – usually arranged by bankers from Genoa and Augsburg. These instruments were especially attractive to that section of the nobility called the hidalgos, which was exempt from most taxes, including those on income from credit bonds.

Meanwhile the rest of the population, already suffering from food-price inflation, could not find work in the cities because no one was investing in manufacturing. Burgos and Toledo went from boom to bust, their wares undercut by imports from China shipped to Europe via Mexico. Once they learned how to tailor their porcelain and silk to meet European tastes, the Chinese produced at scale and ultra-low cost. The Spanish invented global trade only to have it undermine their domestic industry. Urban workers abandoned towns for the countryside and Spain fell back into a feudal state. But rich Spaniards maintained a life of luxury by owning financial assets, claims on the China trade and other forms of property.

REFORMATION AND CAPITALISM
As Spain was raking in treasure from the New World, sparking the Price Revolution, another revolution was brewing – one with far more extensive consequences. In 1517, the German monk Martin Luther published his Ninety-Five Theses in the Hapsburg city of Wittenberg, agitating against corrupt practices of the Catholic Church and hawkers of indulgences such as Jakob Fugger. This protest eventually sparked the Reformation, in which new Protestant faiths challenged the Vatican's writ. And just as Gutenberg's invention of moveable type had made it easy to print coins in bulk, so too it simplified printing pamphlets that spread Protestant ideas everywhere.

The papacy led a Counter-Reformation movement, and the kings of ultra-Catholic Spain were its biggest cheerleaders. Ferdinand and Isabella had already promoted forced conversions of Muslims and Jews, and now they did the same to Protestants throughout the Hapsburg Empire. They levied punitive taxes on regions with Protestant movements, then followed up with military force.

Nowhere did this generate more resistance than in the Low Countries. Several Dutch provinces seceded, creating the Dutch United Provinces. Spain, as the world's foremost power, was already involved in plenty of conflict. But the Reformation led to a new series of debilitating wars of religion at a time when silver was losing its value, and the rulers found themselves awash in coins yet increasingly desperate for money. Spain began to suffer defeats, and none stung more than the loss of the United Provinces in 1581.

Spain's sunset as a global power was mirrored by the rise of the Dutch. Spain had created the first global empire, and its legacy is the Columbian exchange, the establishment of global trade and the existence of Spanish-speaking Latin America. The Dutch went on to create a colonial trading empire too, but one based around what became the world's first capitalist society.

By the early 17th century, Dutch ships had begun attacking the Portuguese in their Asian strongholds, and Dutch raiders commandeered trade in everything from nutmeg to African slaves. They created a world-spanning empire, connecting Batavia (Jakarta) to South Africa to the Caribbean. But there the similarities to Spain end. The United Provinces were not a unified country under a powerful monarch. Their power didn't come from a large population of battle-hardened adventurers. No, the Dutch used finance to catapult themselves into the first rank.

The spread of Italian banking to other cities coincided with a borrowing binge among rulers throughout Europe, emphasised by the Hapsburgs' ties to the Fugger family. Amsterdam emerged as a hotbed for trading these government IOUs, but the same trend was happening from Augsburg to Hamburg. What made Amsterdam different was its policy of toleration.

The Reformation had led to the Low Countries becoming a chequerboard of Catholic and various Protestant communities. The Dutch jurist Hugo Grotius, who was forced into exile for his Calvinist beliefs, published a series of treatises from about 1605 to 1615 arguing that states should be based on rule of law, not raw force. He assumed society would be broadly Christian and saw no benefit in governments interfering with people's personal beliefs. He quickly made the link between freedom of faith and freedom in other spheres, notably commerce.

Such was the spirit guiding the United Dutch Provinces as they emerged from the Spanish grip, and the new nation welcomed Protestant and Jewish refugees from all over Europe. Catholic rulers were obsessed with punishing heresy, throwing even Galileo in jail on the grounds that his arguing the earth revolved around the sun was promoting a "Protestant" belief. In this climate, Amsterdam became a magnet for people of talent. The philosophers Baruch Spinoza and René Descartes did their work in Holland. Less heralded but equally useful people arrived with knowledge of Italian banking.

Later writers, notably Max Weber, argued that Calvinism and other Protestant faiths encouraged a work ethic. If you couldn't be sure of your place in heaven by paying the Catholic Church a tithe, then you needed other signs of salvation, which came to be viewed as hard work and material success in the form of capital, not conspicuous consumption. True or not, the Dutch of the 15th and early 16th centuries certainly fostered a bustling commercial culture.

THE WISSELBANK, THE VOC AND THE BEURS

The proliferation of bonds and coins and the expanding riches of international trade led to growing opportunities for moneylenders and bankers. The Amsterdam Exchange Bank, the Wisselbank, was established in 1609 as a clearing house for merchants dealing in multiple currencies. It was, in a way, Grotius's ideas of rule of law and equality, expressed in the language of money.

The Netherlands was a small, open trading society awash with coins from all over Europe, not to mention many minted by the various provinces. The politics of the United Provinces didn't allow for a single national currency or mint. Debasement became a threat to its prosperity because creditors were receiving back coins of lesser value. That also led to a weakening of the price of money held at banks, versus their value on the street, let alone what they were worth when freshly minted. If creditors were at risk, then so was the entire Dutch economy.

As customers deposited their various coins, the Wisselbank, overseen by the Amsterdam city government, began crediting them in what came to be called "bank money". The Wisselbank guaranteed

The Vereenigde Oostindische
Compagnie held a monopoly
on trade with Japan

to return deposits of whatever currency in the equivalent of freshly minted, high-quality guilders. In other words, the bank guaranteed your deposits would be returned whole, not in some debased manner, and it stuck to that promise. The value of bank money came to enjoy a premium against street prices. This established trust in the bank and in the coinage. Bank money also encouraged people to leave deposits for longer, so the Wisselbank soon branched into lending, to the city government (in secret) and to other banks.

The Dutch had invented the central bank. The Wisselbank, by defending the value of coinage, was turning into the cornerstone of the Amsterdam market. It became the leading bank for all of northern Europe, and the guilder the region's de facto currency.

Central banking was in fact just one of a trio of Dutch innovations that made Amsterdam the world's first global financial centre.

The industrious Dutch set out on risky ventures, both in terms of domestic manufacturing and overseas trade. Christopher Columbus had been financed largely by the Spanish government. The United Provinces was not a big nation-state, but a federation of small states, not in the business of financing private adventures. So the Dutch created their second innovation: the company. Specifically, the joint-stock, limited-liability company.

The United East India Company, or Vereenigde Oostindische Compagnie (VOC), was founded in 1602 with a charter giving it a monopoly on Dutch trade in Asia. Joint-stock companies up to this point could be very big (the British East India Company, founded in 1600, would become a gigantic enterprise) but they were private, short-term pools of partners' money. The VOC was different. It achieved vast scale by allowing all Amsterdam residents to subscribe and become shareholders. Ownership of financial instruments was now open to the urban middle class. In turn, it came to operate the biggest commercial fleet in the world and dozens of offices in Asia, not to mention a monopoly on trade with Japan.

Typical of the era, the initial plan for VOC shareholders was to allow shareholders to withdraw their money after ten years. But financing long-haul sea voyages, fighting the Portuguese and establishing colonies was a long-term and expensive business. When 1612 rolled around, the company managers decided not to allow people to liquidate their positions. As a result, shareholders who wanted their money back had but one recourse – to sell their stake to someone else.

And so was born the third Dutch innovation: the stock market. Even before the VOC managers officially announced their decision to sustain the company, a market had developed for trading VOC stock and other company stocks. The frenzy was such that the city erected a covered beurs (bourse) where trading could take place.

The stock market invited a kind of speculative frenzy which had never been seen. Along with this evolved the gamut of tools familiar to a Wall Street trader: hedging options, prime brokerage, and the language of bears and bulls. By the late 17th century, such was the pace and weirdness of this speculation that the first contemporary to write about it named his book "Confusion of Confusions".

But this masked what was really going on: the rise of a new class of person who gained (and lost) fortunes based purely on taking risk. Until now, fortunes required owning large estates or big trading companies, which themselves succeeded by conquering far-off lands. On the Dam, though, wealth became open to people other than static aristocrats.

It could be lost overnight as well: in 1636-37, a mania for tulip bulbs created the first stock-market bubble and bust. But the fallout, although ruinous for foolish investors, did nothing to stop Amsterdam's love affair with finance. If anything, society doubled down.

The power of Amsterdam's finance industry was in combining these innovations so they reinforced one another. The Wisselbank gradually came to accept VOC shares as collateral against loans. At first the traffic was one way; borrowers used VOC equity to finance a loan, trusting the Wisselbank to return their shares in full, assuming they paid back the loan on time. But then the traffic became two-way as people started borrowing from the Wisselbank in order to buy VOC shares. Now the stock market and the central bank were connected via exchange based on guilders – without the government having decreed anything.

The link between banking and the stock market rapidly accelerated the supply of credit, which underpinned the rapid expansion of Dutch commerce and empire. To be sure, the creation of financial markets led to excesses. When the tulip craze went bust, plenty of people lost their shirts, but it didn't impact the stability of Amsterdam's market. There was a bubble in tulip prices because people went mad over something of no real intrinsic value, but there was never a bubble in VOC stock.

FINANCIAL CENTRE

This is what the Spanish never understood: power was no longer about who owned the most coins or land in a zero-sum world of finite wealth. It was about who could create and receive credit, and by whose rules. Money was still an abstraction, but the token representing it had changed from something physical, like a silver coin, into something intangible: the balance between a bank's liabilities (in the form of deposits and reserves) and its assets (loans).

By the end of the 17th century, the Dutch – without any Incan bullion hoards to steal – had amassed the most assets and savings in the world. They eclipsed Spain by using bank money to support complex, multi-generational ventures and indulged in risky speculation to conjure fortunes.

And, most mysteriously of all, the Dutch could borrow cheaply. Interest rates in Amsterdam had fallen as low as 3% for trusted borrowers like the VOC and the government. Borrowing rates for European monarchs were 8% or more because kings were regular defaulters. The Dutch stadtholders, lacking a single person with absolute power, prioritised repaying debts on time. Just as the Wisselbank earned the trust of depositors, the Dutch government earned the trust of lenders. The yield on Dutch bonds fell steadily from 20% in 1517 to 4% in 1700.

To be sure, the Dutch empire was also built on exploitation, from conquering Asian entrepôts to committing the atrocities of the slave trade. Financial success was dependent on the VOC's profitability, which in turn required brute force and the support of what was then the world's most powerful navy. But whereas the Spanish ended up recreating a Roman Empire-like reliance on booty and conquest, the Dutch invented a new kind of economy, one rooted in the rule of law (at least at home), the welcoming of talent and financial innovation. The VOC would operate for 200 years, but never had to issue new equity: starting in the 1630s, it relied on borrowing. The Dutch economy ran on the rails of finance, making the United Provinces the first capitalist society.

Capitalism brought many benefits, not least enabling a small trading nation to support a planetary network of colonies, ships and companies. But capitalism had its dark side, and not just for the Africans ruthlessly shackled in Dutch slave ships or native workers indentured to their colonial plantations. For while the Dutch surpassed the Spanish with their facility with money, they couldn't avoid the trap of financialisation.

By the 1670s, finance was driving out commerce based on physical labour. Amsterdam had become the world's first global financial centre, creating investment funds to channel its wealth. Dutch investors lost interest in financing Dutch enterprises, even the VOC. It was far more lucrative, and much safer, to invest in property and bonds. The thrusting era of Erasmus (humanist), Rembrandt (art), Vermeer (art) and Leeuwenhoek (microbiology), a time of bourgeois

ascendance, thrift and industriousness, gave way to growing inequality and a decline in local production. The vast reserves of Dutch capital shifted overseas, where returns were higher. Ordinary Dutch – the local burgher class that had built the country – slipped into poverty. Towns depopulated. Local businesses shut. The need for solace turned gin production into the single domestic growth industry.

For all of the financial innovation in the United Provinces, something intrinsic about money had not changed.

From the ancient Greek agora to the Medici family to the burghers of Amsterdam, money has led to new forms of cooperation and exchange. It has fostered a cosmopolitan elite who value useful commercial relationships over tribe or religion. Their currencies – drachmas, florins, guilders – are the glue that led to ever-widening networks of cooperation, allowing people to build world-spanning companies and infrastructure. But social solidarity? That's something else.

The Dutch Golden Age ended in 1672 when the nation found itself at war with England, France and several German duchies at the same time. The only way to fend off the advancing armies was to breach the dykes and flood the country. Holland retained its role as a financial and technological centre and a colonial power, but the local economy never really recovered. By now the elite had decoupled their assets from the country and there was no appetite to reinvest domestically. The Netherlands still owned the world's greatest pool of capital, but by 1700 it was mostly invested in its great commercial rival: Great Britain.

Now impoverished, the need for solace turned gin production into the only domestic growth industry

FAKE MONEY

The first coins in Lydia were followed by the first counterfeits. Since then issuers have always fought against fraud. But counterfeiting is not treated like ordinary scams or robbery. Rulers have always regarded it as a crime against the state. The penalties are always severe: hanging, drawing and quartering, burning at the stake.

Thirteenth-century Chinese mints posted armed guards around the mulberry trees that produced the raw material for the world's first paper money, ready to mete out justice on the spot. Even General George Washington, while fighting the American Revolution, suggested torturing a couple of suspected counterfeiters to find out if they were British agents out to destroy the American currency.

Governments have been the most prominent counterfeiters, using forgery as a tactic to destabilise enemies. In fact, coins and paper money aren't necessary for counterfeiting: commodity-money will do.

In the 17th century, African kingdoms like Benin and Congo were resisting the European-led slave trade. These realms relied on cowry shells for their currency. So Portuguese privateers gathered a huge haul of shells from around the Indian Ocean and dumped them in Africa, devastating the local economies and undermining resistance to the slave trade. The Dutch pulled a similar stunt in the Indian Ocean, the shocks of which reverberated as far away as China.

But paper money has been especially susceptible to plagiarism, and the effects can be serious. Alves dos Reis perpetrated a massive fraud against the Bank of Portugal in 1925. He faked approvals from the central bank to print notes for the purpose of lending to a commercial group investing in Angola. He duped a British printer into making the notes, even reusing serial numbers from actual Portuguese money. Reis created almost 1% of the circulation of Portuguese escudos, pocketing 25% for himself with the aim of using it to buy a stake in the Bank of Portugal itself to cover his tracks. The scam was discovered and Reis was eventually jailed for 20 years, but the low level of trust in Portuguese affairs meant the central bank's officials were long suspected of complicity.

The most notorious counterfeiting plot was Operation Bernhard, an attempt by Nazi Germany to forge British banknotes and thereby undermine its economy. Later the aims changed to financing military and espionage operations, such as the 1943 commando raid that freed Benito Mussolini from an Allied prison.

The Nazis used Jewish experts held in Sachsenhausen concentration camp to forge both British and American notes. They printed as much as GBP300m, much of it of high enough quality to use. As the war closed, the Nazis planned to murder the prisoners, but some mishaps delayed the slaughter and American troops liberated the prisoners. British currency experts were astounded by the quality of the prisoners' work.

09

REVOLUTION

In England, the Glorious
Revolution marked its
passage from peripheral
to global power

Money is both a reflection of the times and a shaper of trends. As societies change the way they use money, it influences how people think and what they value. Yet for all of the big trends in history – the Islamic Golden Age, the Renaissance or the Age of Discovery, for example – there is no Age of Money.

Money is one of the original technologies that defined civilisation. There's no Age of Money just as there's no Age of Food or Era of Energy. It's always present, shape-shifting to serve the moment. It's a metaphor, a thing that represents something else, and the nature of that other thing tends to change. Yet everyone knows when they have money – and when they don't. Once money began to circulate as currency, it became the primary benchmark for status and allowed people to take stock of their own place in the world.

And money's tangling with faith, government and technology led to one upheaval in fortune after another. In 17th-century Europe, new attitudes and beliefs came to redefine money. Speculation, even about fripperies such as tulip bulbs, involved new ways of thinking about the future. Just as Buddhism and Christianity helped broaden people's ideas about the possible, new techniques based on risk revolutionised attitudes towards the days to come.

While the Dutch were engaged in financial speculation, aristocrats enjoyed spending their wealth on fashion, prostitutes and, most of all, gambling. At Versailles, where King Louis XIV kept noblemen in enforced seclusion, the rich acquired a taste for *risque*. Risk also interested serious philosophers, such as Blaise Pascal, Pierre de Fermat, Sir Isaac Newton and Christiaan Huygens, who applied mathematics to games.

Huygens's "De Alea", published in 1657, established probability theory, giving people a way to peer into the future. *Risque* could be calculated for the gambling den, or the stock market, or for completely new industries, like insurance. A prominent English businessman, Nicholas Barbon, responded to the Great London Fire of

1666 with a massive building program combined with the first fire insurance, using statistical calculations to sell protection against future calamity.

As European power and influence – especially British – extended across the world, the West experienced or fostered an ever-increasing number of revolutions. The tempo of change quickened, and nothing is more malleable than money.

THE GLORIOUS REVOLUTION OF 1688

The Dutch had nearly lost everything in 1672 when they barely survived foreign invasions. Although the merchants of Amsterdam were happy to do business with national rivals, the town stewards or stadtholders regarded France as their greatest enemy: authoritarian, powerful and Catholic.

England was now under the rule of another Catholic, King James II, who had aims to mimic the French monarchy. He shared the prevailing attitude among most European rulers, viewing wealth as finite and physical.

The idea of England falling permanently into the Catholic camp was therefore not just a political threat to the Dutch, who knew that arbitrary monarchy would also snuff out finance, given the tendency among kings to default.

Fortunately, the Dutch weren't alone in this fear. Many English shared their concern in what was still a majority-Protestant nation whose people had already endured a civil war to depose an earlier Catholic monarch, King Charles I. Moreover, England's merchants and goldsmiths enjoyed unrivalled freedoms in a country that was becoming stable, prosperous and capable of pursuing its own foreign adventures – all at risk should the country and its finances be subject to an arbitrary ruler.

The chief stadtholder of the United Provinces was Willem III, Prince of Orange, who was also related to James II: his wife, Mary, was James's daughter. The family link was enough of a fig leaf to justify a plot Willem hatched with English Protestant allies to invade England and depose James.

For such a small country to invade England required more than partners. It required money. Willem relied on the financial power of Amsterdam to borrow what he required, at 3% interest, far below the 8% James had to pay. Moreover, Willem could borrow from the market. James had to rely on personal loans or taxes to secure his funding.

Willem financed a powerful navy and an army of mostly foreign mercenaries which he was able to land (with the luck of a favourable wind at the navy's back). The clash was brief, and when most of his men deserted, James fled to France. In late 1688, Willem – now "William" – and Mary were proclaimed joint sovereigns of England.

The invasion locked in an English-Dutch alliance, although for the United Provinces this victory was temporary because it now suffered constant attack by France. Amsterdam's market enabled the country to finance a resistance for decades. Eventually, however, spending so much on unproductive warfare caused Holland's fortunes to decline permanently. In contrast, 1688 became known in England as the Glorious Revolution, marking its passage from peripheral to global power.

What made it so was a combination of changes brought about by the invasion. First, King William was a smart politician but a cold, unlikeable personality who relied on the charm of Queen Mary to win social acceptance. He was also a foreigner who had been allowed to invade in order to see off tyranny. William's rule would be limited, with Parliament playing a much bigger role. He brought with him Dutch notions of tolerance, but more fundamentally, the distribution of power meant that no faction could ever dominate, nor stifle radical change. The rising tide of new ideas – from the uplands of mathematics and physics, calls for free trade and critiques of religion, down to

the swamp's demands for cards, dice, fashion and speculation – had no dyke keep them at bay.

Those new ideas would be applied fastest in the world of money. The cost of warfare kept rising more than what the government could generate by raising taxes. Borrowing at 8% in such large amounts quickly emptied the exchequer's coffers.

First William approached the City – the money markets – for a loan. He was the first monarch to do so. But the proceeds were immediately spent and the wars dragged on. He needed a way to bring the cost of borrowing down to Amsterdam rates. Instead of tying borrowing to the monarch, William relinquished this power to Parliament.

Now it was not a capricious king asking for money; it was the nation. Moreover, once Parliament began to borrow, creating the national debt, it found it could borrow in perpetuity rather than relying on short-term quick fixes, which meant it could borrow at lower cost. Lower interest rates and rising liquidity created a market in which trusted businessmen could also borrow for the long term, giving rise to banks and insurance companies that based their operations on calculated risk.

King William's ascent had been accompanied by a change in political fortunes, with the Tories out and the modernising Whigs in. These leaders were now able to push through plans that had languished under James II's rule. In 1694, two entrepreneurs, Michael Godfrey and William Paterson, proposed the establishment of a national bank that could lend money to the government.

The City of London, a square mile within Greater London, had since ancient times been designated a place where merchants could conduct business unimpeded. It was here where the Bank of England was established as a private holding company, but with exclusive rights to hold royal deposits.

Godfrey and Paterson saw that over time this national bank could also manage government debt and facilitate payments for trade with bills of exchange. By borrowing in longer terms and generating liquidity, they would make government debt attractive, and market forces would push interest rates down, benefiting both the government and private borrowers. William liked the idea, and chartered the Bank of England.

The Bank of England represents more than just yet another marker along the highway of financial history. Its unique combination of Crown and City represents a truce between authorities seeking to monopolise power over money and merchants masking their dealings. William made a deal with the businessmen. Commercial banks could go about lending and borrowing – making private money – and have say in the management of public finances. In return they would continue to support the government's borrowing needs and accept a degree of government oversight. The writer Felix Martin calls this the "great monetary settlement", and it would underpin stable, regulated finance into the 20th century.

But it would take a long time for the newly chartered Bank of England to develop the money market. In the meantime, William faced a more immediate crisis: he was running out of coins.

Britain was awash with a variety of low-value coins made without any standards. Business was done using a confusing mix of pennies, guineas, farthings, shillings, crowns and so on. These coins were still made using hammers, as if this were ancient Greece, with a large portion of coins either "clipped" (debased) or counterfeit. The goldsmiths who produced much of this dodgy money were also the country's primary moneylenders, as there was no professional banker class.

Since the days of Queen Elizabeth I, England had gone through several "great recoinage" campaigns, introducing "milled" or mechanised printing, but with poor results. By 1690, much of the currency was worth only half its face value.

After the currency collapsed in 1695, Isaac Newton was named Warden to the Mint in England

William called for another great recoinage. The Royal Mint set about replacing the country's coinage with new, quality silver coins. But this effort fell short because the Mint could not stabilise prices between silver, gold and other commodities. In 1695 the currency collapsed, leaving the government broke, so William turned to Isaac Newton for help, naming the famous scholar warden to the Mint the following year.

Newton's efforts were a success because he understood the bimetallic system of currency was unstable. He thought the government should rest its finances on gold, and to that end he coined the first pound sterling that contained a pound's worth of gold.

Newton's pound was favoured by merchants, and though it was too valuable for everyday transactions, it eventually put British coinage on firm footing. Over time, the pound would serve as the bedrock of the British-led gold standard. But that was for the future. In the meantime, William and his allies still faced a financial crisis.

Questioning and free thought were a vital part of the Glorious Revolution, and the crisis led people to ask why the government was being brought to its knees because it had run out of silver and gold. Weren't these just ordinary commodities? What made these so special?

It was Nicholas Barbon, the London real-estate mogul, who gave the unsettling answer: nothing. Nothing made them special. Money, he wrote, was "an imaginary value made by law for the conveniency of exchange."

Money wasn't about its intrinsic value. This is something merchants had grasped since the Italian Rennaissance. But for most people, including rulers, currency was tied to bullion or land. The idea of using something like paper to represent it was outlandish.

But no matter. Crisis demanded innovation: giving the Bank of England the privilege of issuing banknotes.

EUROPE'S PAPER REVOLUTION

China had used paper money since the ninth century, making it a fixture under the Tang, Song, Mongol (Yuan) and Ming dynasties. Private merchants had invented paper money, recognising its usefulness for payments and investments, but the Chinese state tended to muscle in, at times monopolising paper printing – and always overdoing it. Successive dynasties collapsed thanks to inflation and monetary collapse. Chinese rulers relied on brute force to make people use state-backed paper, such as by requiring taxes be paid in paper instead of giving capital markets free reign to circulate money.

Nonetheless it was a massive innovation, one that recognised the value of money was not the thing itself – not the silver or the paper – but the belief that the rules defining its value would be widely accepted as good.

The first European government to issue paper money was Sweden's private Stockholms Banco. Sweden lacked the gold and silver to back up a national currency. It had copper, but this was a base metal, so hefty quantities were required to make large units. The government issued giant sheets of copper, some of which ended up weighing 44 lb, which was far too cumbersome for merchants to handle.

Johan Palmstruch, a banker who had previously worked in Amsterdam, suggested the establishment of something like the Wisselbank to the monarch. He was appointed the bank's director, and in 1661 he took his mandate one step further and issued paper notes, meant to be exchangeable for copper upon demand. Paper notes were instantly popular – too popular. The bank issued more paper than it had bullion reserves to cover, and in 1668 it collapsed. Palmstruch spent almost the entirety of the rest of his life in jail.

Despite this cautionary tale, the emerging banker class in the City of London was confident they could manage things better. After all, the Bank of England was to operate as a commercial, for-profit entity rather than serving the state's whim. The bank was not the first institution in England to issue notes, but it was the first to so backed by royal reserves. Its first notes were issued in denominations of Isaac Newton's pounds sterling, with the GBP symbol (£) derived from libra, the Roman basic unit of weight.

The bank's stewards always prioritised meeting redemptions of notes for gold, and from that basis laid the groundwork to become the most influential financial institution in the world.

This private model came to be followed by most other countries, but not until after several disastrous attempts at more state-directed versions were made. Most famous among these is France. The Duke of Orleans, the powerful regent to the boy king Louis XV, liked the ideas put to him by John Law, a Scotsman with a scandalous background (duels, debts, affairs). Law argued that a royal absolute state should command a national bank that printed national paper money.

The king decreed in 1716 the establishment of what became Banque Générale, with Law at its head. Law lobbied to have the bank nationalised and set about issuing banknotes backed by royal gold coins. As with the Swedish example, there were never enough reserves, but Law thought all the system needed was public confidence in the king as the final backstop. Law didn't see the value in having public banks act as counterweights to the king.

Matters really got out of control when Law set up the Mississippi Company, ostensibly a VOC knock-off meant to exploit France's holdings in North America, with revenues meant to pay national debts. With a combination of hype and deceit, he sparked a frenzy in Paris as the elite sought to cash in on this "sure thing". The swindle soon attracted investors from London too. For a while, prices of everything were going up, and the French coined the term millionaire.

It was all smoke and mirrors, though – or, as one unhappy investor put it, "Shit shares and wind trade" (as recounted by historian Niall Ferguson). For a time, Law tried to prop up the use of banknotes by tinkering with their exchange rates. As more people cashed in Banque Générale notes, he sought to ban the export of gold and silver from France. But if the Mongols couldn't succeed in using violence to enforce the value of their money, what chance did John Law have? When the Mississippi Company bubble finally burst, it revealed the French state to be utterly bankrupt.

Both Palmstruch and Law failed to realise two things. First, balance matters: putting too much power in the hands of the government only led to the sort of abuse that the Ming Dynasty had indulged. Second, so did attitude: it wasn't enough to have royal backing to make people want to use banknotes. The Bank of England's stewards, on the other hand, realised trust had to be earned. The Bank – along with its sibling, the Bank of Scotland – depended on many shareholders who provided a broad capital base. It was this well-funded, well-managed approach that earned the confidence of the people.

Although Palmstruch and Law are often portrayed as villains, they were also financial innovators who thought paper money would help governments finance themselves. Europeans had no experience with paper money and no knowledge of the Chinese story. Each new issue of money was a voyage into unknown territory.

But gradually the Bank of England earned enough credibility to extend into commercial loans. It became a lender to the many "country banks" popping up throughout Great Britain to help finance economic activity. In turn, it became the model that other countries looked to, and by the end of the 18th century, more than 20 nations had set up central banks issuing paper money.

The Bank of England really proved itself at war, however. France was England's greatest rival, one with a centralised state and a big population. The French Revolution posed a new threat, especially when it fell under Napoleon Bonaparte, who fused revolutionary fever with old-fashioned dreams of conquest.

By the end of the 18th century, London had become the biggest financial centre, full of highly talented immigrants. The most prominent of these was Nathan Rothschild, the Frankfurt-born member of a Jewish family with offices run by siblings across Europe. The Rothschilds learned how to take advantage of variations of prices in different countries for the same foreign-exchange transaction. This is called arbitrage. It requires having information that others lack, and the Rothschilds, with their international connections, had the most information. Nathan Rothschild soon dominated the London money markets.

In 1815, the Duke of Wellington was leading the military campaign against Napoleon. He needed money to pay his troops and suppliers across all of Europe, in currencies they'd accept locally. He couldn't just hand out Bank of England notes. He needed gold.

The Bank of England provided stability, both to Great Britain as well as to the rest of the world

With a printing press in Philadelphia, Benjamin Franklin was the true father of paper money

Rothschild manipulated his extensive network to mobilise finances wherever payments were required. Information was only valuable if it could be acted upon. He used the London banking market to provide loans to allied governments or help them issue bonds in London.

After Wellington prevailed at the Battle of Waterloo, England became the world's unchallenged power – and the City its engine. Rothschild, along with other immigrant families such as the Warburgs and the Barings, went on to dominate international finance. And in future, he would only underwrite foreign borrowings denominated in sterling.

The Bank of England provided stability, both to Great Britain and to the rest of the world. London's money markets were unrivalled for their liquidity and breadth. The Bank of England's steadfast commitment to letting depositors convert money back to gold transformed gold, over time, into the world currency.

This was sometimes unpopular with politicians, who might have preferred money be printed in accordance with their whims rather than with the supply of gold in the Bank's vaults. But this discipline maintained the pre-eminence of the City and the Bank, enabling them to underpin the British Empire and the Industrial Revolution.

THE AMERICAN REVOLUTION

For a long time in the City of London, only merchants used banknotes, be they issued by the Bank of England, by other banks or by goldsmith guilds. Banknote denominations were too high for anything but large-scale activities. Coins remained Britain's leading form of currency. The failures in Stockholm and Paris put the brakes on paper money in Europe.

The first place to embrace paper money as a way of life was the United States. The British colonies in North America were always starved of money and short of bullion. The Spanish silver piece of eight –

known in North America as the Spanish dollar – and other foreign coins circulated, but at volatile rates of exchange. As early as 1690, before the creation of the Bank of England or John Law's Banque Générale, the Massachusetts Bay Colony produced paper bills to finance a military expedition to Canada.

The true father of paper money is not Chinese or European: it's Benjamin Franklin, who in Philadelphia operated a printing press. He put this to work on his almanacs, pamphlets and books – and to print cash on behalf of the colony of Pennsylvania.

Colonial Americans were wary of paper money, which people knew wasn't backed by enough bullion. States printed notes anyway, to the extent that British authorities deemed it a threat to the pound. In 1751, Parliament banned the use of paper money in the colonies, a precursor to later Stamp Acts and other economic penalties that fuelled the anger that would lead to the American Revolution.

Franklin was at the forefront of this nascent, revolutionary society. As a printer he shaped the national ethos based on thrift, hard work, education, self-government and commitment to the liberal ideas of the Enlightenment. His almanacs advised Americans that "Time is money", and that "Early to bed and early to rise, makes a man healthy, wealthy and wise."

Franklin's writings on the necessity of paper money were put into action during the Revolution. The United States was the first nation to win a major war financed solely on the issuance of paper notes – that is, on money that had become completely untied from any commodity. Not silver, not gold, not tobacco leaves, not cacao beans, not cowry shells: the Continental dollar was first issued in 1775 purely on the authority of the revolutionary government.

Of course, "not worth a Continental" entered the American lexicon because these notes depreciated to nothing. Revolutionary governments are better known for turmoil than economic stability, and to be sure, the Americans printed far too much.

THE INDUSTRIAL REVOLUTION

The other innovation in American money was the nation's adoption of the decimal system. Russia actually pioneered a decimal system as early as 1535, when one Novgorod rouble was divided into 100 denga, and a century later, Peter the Great revamped the system with kopecs. Russia's arrangement would last until the 20th century, but it wasn't complete: the rouble continued to exist alongside other non-decimal currencies.

The idea of a rationally formed standard for currencies didn't take hold elsewhere, though, because other European monarchs weren't about to mimic anything from backwards Russia. Besides, the more confusing the system of currencies, the easier it was for monarchs to manipulate it.

But the Americans, with their mass issuance of paper money, needed a system that everyone could use, as befit a democratic revolution. That meant it needed to be organised in a user-friendly manner. Decimalisation also befit a new republic founded upon the scientific ideas of the Enlightenment. Thomas Jefferson came up with the idea of calling one-hundredth of a dollar a "cent" and a tenth a "dime" based on Latin precursors.

Finally, the Americans couldn't swallow copying British high-value coins with names like crowns and sovereigns, given their royal meanings. The widespread circulation of the Spanish peso (or thaler, the leading coin in the Spanish Hapsburg Empire) made it natural for the revolutionaries to name their currency the dollar.

From the start, then, money was a symbol of the American experiment. And as in no other society in the world, money and banking would be hotly contested political issues. The depreciation of the Continental dollar left a bad taste. This only worsened when the Second Bank of the United States, which lasted from 1816 to 1836, held too little coin reserve and lent too widely. The ensuing recession when it suffered a run helped propel the anti-bank populist Andrew Jackson to the presidency, and America would not establish a central bank until 1913.

The association of decimalisation with revolution put other governments off adopting metric standards. The exception was the world's other great revolutionary power: France. The Ancien Régime had gone bankrupt from John Law's Mississippi Company scandal. French Revolutionaries, lacking coins and seeing the American example, immediately turned to paper. The National Assembly issued *assignats* in 1789. At first these were backed by confiscated church and crown properties, which was more than the Americans ever had. But as always, the government's needs outran its collateral. The French overprinted and their *assignats* lost all value.

Napoleon, who seized power in 1799, hated paper money and returned the government to relying on metal coins and bills of exchange. But he advanced the use of the metric system. The early Republic had adopted a metric system of currency in 1795, replacing the livre with the franc, subdivided by 100 centimes.

This was in keeping with a movement among French revolutionaries to adapt the metric system to all weights and measures in order to advance a new, scientific society. They replaced a convoluted series of medieval measurements with litres, metres and grams. In their zeal, the revolutionaries got carried away. Right angles should be 100 degrees, not 90; days should have 10 hours, not 24; and so on. Napoleon got rid of the more ridiculous changes, but he maintained the idea of the French Revolution as a civilisational package that he wanted to export across Europe, of which decimal money and the metric system were a part.

Just as the introduction of coins in ancient Greece had

changed the way people thought and the values they promoted, so too did decimalisation and the metric system change European thought. The scientists and inventors developing the technologies of industry needed reliable ways to measure everything from temperatures to air pressure to electrical currents. Numbering led to mathematics, which were then applied to a widening array of fields, from economics to law.

Standardising measurements girded the emerging scientific and industrial upheavals. In Britain, banking shifted to support the needs of the Industrial Revolution. Only capital markets could enable inventions such as the steam engine to deploy at scale. London's financiers were not placing their bets on tulip bulbs or East India Company shares: beginning in the 1690s, they invested in joint-stock companies that had patented scientific inventions they hoped would yield riches.

Britain's industrialists currency embraced metric measurements but Britain resisted decimalisation until 1971, when Parliament replaced all the pennies and farthings and guineas with a pound made up of 100 pence. But otherwise, British banking led the way and was indispensable to the advancement of the Industrial Revolution. Without agile capital markets, there is no way assets could have been shifted so readily from traditional agriculture to industry, or from rural areas to factory towns.

On both sides of the Atlantic, new currencies transformed society. In Britain, the demands of the Industrial Revolution could not be met by government-controlled banks. A vast and specialised banking and insurance sector arose to meet the needs of industrialists. For the first time, private banks overtook governments when it came to credit creation or asset allocation. Financial power shifted from the Crown to the City and was increasingly represented by paper money.

The circulation of paper notes finally outstripped coins in Britain in 1776. This was the year when Adam Smith published his "Inquiry into the Nature and Causes of the Wealth of Nations", in which he argued that the value of money wasn't about gold itself, but the amount of labour for which it could be exchanged. It was the "invisible hand" of many private exchanges that drove wealth, not royal diktat.

Until that time, coins and paper notes had been associated with government power, from Alexander the Great and Kublai Khan to Isabella and Ferdinand. But now money was becoming the instrument of democracy and private enterprise. The "great monetary settlement" begun with the Bank of England had yielded its bounty.

CURRENCY AS ART

Banknotes have evolved into more than national symbols. At their finest, they are highly accomplished works of art.

The greenback may be the world's dominant currency, but its look and feel hasn't changed much since it was first introduced in 1862. American notes all feature presidents.

In comparison, the rest of the world's currency is vivid.

From the seashells of the Aruba florin to the slave breaking his chains on the Zambian 5,000-kwacha note, the art on money is serving the same purpose as Alexander's stamping his image on his coins: as propaganda. But what is the story being advertised?

When the Bank of England began issuing notes with the likeness of Queen Elizabeth II, it marked a shift away from symbols in favour of regents, at least in Britain. The 20th century was the era of showcasing presidents and kings, founding fathers (almost always dads) and independence leaders, from Gandhi to Mao.

This may be starting to change. The banknotes of many countries printed in the 21st century favour images promoting other values. Switzerland's SFr50 note of 2016 replaced famous personalities with a hand, representing all Swiss people. Canada's CUSD5 note portrays children playing ice hockey.

Others emphasise a country's natural beauty, such as Bermuda's 2-dollar note of 2010 showing colourful birds and flowers, or Argentina's 500-peso note of 2016 illustrated with pumas.

Another theme is a country's industry, as shown by Scotland's 50-pound note of 2007 that shows the inventor and writer Sir Walter Scott, with a Falkirk wheel portrayed on the obverse.

Others boast of their arts, be it Israeli poet Nathan Alterman on the 200-shekel note; Higuchi Ichiyo, a 19th-century Japanese author, on the JPY5,000 note; or Mexico's 500-peso bill with painters Diego Rivera and Frida Kahlo on either side.

In Britain, banking shifted to support the Industrial Revolution, fuelled by paper money

10
GOLD

The problem with a gold standard, of course, is that it is dependent upon the supply of gold mined from the ground

E urope's 19th century began amid the turmoil of the Napoleonic wars. But economically, the year 1800 was as stolid as in previous eras. A small elite of aristocrats, clerics and merchants owned almost all the wealth, mostly through inheritance. When Napoleon scrapped the printing of paper *assignats* and returned France to metal coins, prices instantly returned to pre-revolutionary levels, as though nothing had happened. Only massive shocks such as Spain's dumping of New-World gold could impact prices in a world with so little growth.

Yet within a short time, Europe changed. Politically it became peaceful and stable. The British led a coalition, financed by the London money markets, that finally defeated Napoleon in 1815. The ensuing peace allowed European monarchs and merchants to accelerate empire-building abroad, in Africa and Asia, further tipping the scales of wealth from East to West.

At the same time, European economics became dynamic. Although colonialism generated wealth, it didn't, by itself, drive faster economic growth rates. By 1815, however, the ideas of the Enlightenment were powering both advances in science and ideas about how civilised nations should govern themselves, notably through reason.

This applied most of all to matters of money, with the Bank of England at the centre of affairs. The institution soon eclipsed Amsterdam's Wisselbank and became a different kind of central bank: a lender of last resort, upon which the rest of the world came to depend.

National banks, including those of England and Scotland, at first held their reserve assets in gold and silver bullion. As international commerce expanded on the back of both more colonies and general peace, these national banks began swapping bills of exchange. Originally these were just bilateral transactions between, say, the Bank of England and the French central bank, and were conducted purely to facilitate private commerce. But then, as always happens with successful money instruments, a secondary market developed, making these bills of exchange a form of tradable currency. This became the modern foreign-exchange market.

Such markets had origins in the Italian city-states, were promoted by the Wisselbank, and reached their apogee in 18th- and 19th-century London and Paris. These were the centres with the most liquid markets, the greatest variety of borrowers and lenders, and the most attractive lending and deposit rates.

Commercial banks operating in these city centres used short-term deposits to extend longer-term foreign loans. Money was becoming a time machine, allocating resources into the future.

In London, however, this system transformed into a system of credit issued by the Bank of England itself, which amassed the leading portfolio of foreign-exchange reserves. In effect, it became the primary banker to other banks, including foreign ones.

Why England? Partly because of its longer history running a quasi-private central bank, but also because it had adhered to the gold standard for far longer than others. A single international standard made it easier to transact, and the Bank of England found it could boost its gold reserves with interest-bearing bills of exchange or other financial assets – that is, Bank-issued paper notes – by promising their convertibility into gold upon demand. The Bank of England earned the trust of the international market.

The problem with a gold standard, of course, is that it depends upon the supply of gold mined from the ground. This problem seemed to resolve itself, however, thanks to major gold finds in California, Australia and South Africa, all territories in which British merchants could operate with ease.

Gradually, the Old Lady of Threadneedle Street – as the Bank became known, from its City address – developed public responsibilities. After an initial period of multiple note issuers, Parliament eventually

gave the Bank a monopoly on printing paper money. This gave the Bank scale, not just nationally but in the City – which is to say, internationally.

Its discount rate (the interest it paid to other banks to hold their reserves) became so influential that the Bank of England became the setter of short-term interest rates throughout the financial system. Although Bank of England notes were based on the supply of precious metals, the central bank lay at the heart of a system of private banks, which could extend their own credit regardless of how much or how little bullion they held.

This position led Scottish journalist Walter Bagehot to describe the Bank as the "lender of last resort" in his famous book "Lombard Street: A Description of the Money Market" (1873). In other words, whenever there was an emergency in liquidity that threatened the money markets, the Bank of England, with its vast reserves and expertise, was expected to step in and provide the monies to prevent an unruly bank collapse.

The Bank, through a long period of trial and error, came to accept this duty. It was, after all, already using its market operations to maintain sterling's parity to gold at the rate of GBP3, 17 shillings and 10.5p per ounce, the rate originally set by Isaac Newton in 1696.

The beauty of the Bank of England's paper notes was how easily these could be used to adjust the supply of money, based on how much the Old Lady chose to print. Money was becoming a tool used by central banks to manage the economy, in the spirit of the Enlightenment. The British economist David Ricardo observed as early as 1817, "It is not necessary that paper should be payable in specie to secure its value, it is only necessary that its quantity should be regulated."

THE ASCENT OF BRITISH CAPITAL
Britain enjoyed a long golden age, which peaked from the railway boom of the 1840s into the 1870s. This period saw the emergence of factory towns throughout England and Scotland, and coal-mining towns in England and Wales. Although society was rife with stratification, the working classes prospered and a middle class emerged. Nothing epitomised Victorian-

era British confidence like the 1851 Crystal Palace Exhibition, which became the first of an ongoing series of world fairs.

Britain's long period of stability went hand in hand with the Industrial Revolution, which began in Britain before extending to France, the Low Countries, Germany and America. The Industrial Revolution involved harnessing new technologies, powered by steam and hydraulics, to mechanise the exploitation of natural resources.

At first, in the 18th century, these technologies were applied to textiles, but by the 1840s they had led to the invention of locomotives, steamships, blast furnaces and advances in communications such as the telegraph. (The first transatlantic telegraph line connected London and New York in 1858 in order to transmit currency information, which is why even today foreign-exchange traders call the sterling-dollar rate "cable".) Along with access to foreign raw materials and an influx of new fortunes, the mechanisation of industry forever transformed British society.

The Bank of England and its gold standard gave this era only the veneer of conservative stability; beneath the surface, growth rates accelerated, from no more than 1% per year in the 18th century to 2% or more in the 19th. Those numbers imply that people experienced dramatic shifts in their lifetimes regarding jobs, employment and living standards. Most obvious, however, was the growing differential between the haves and the have-nots.

In the early decades of high rates of British growth, with most people still working farms, the degree of change in inequality went unnoticed. But the waxing of financialisation that had hollowed out the Spanish and Dutch bourgeoisie occurred in Britain too. And the concentrated misery of the working class in the factories was more visible.

In 1867 Karl Marx published "Das Kapital", in which he argued capitalism was based on the unfair exploitation of labour, abetted by a system of government

Karl Marx argued capitalism was based on the exploitation of labour on behalf of the elite

that protected private property and the means of production on behalf of a small, privileged elite. Money, always political, was getting polemical.

Beginning in the 1870s, the era of British dominance began to unravel. Others learned to mimic British technology. America and a recently unified Germany quickly became industrial rivals. As British industry exited its high-growth era, British investment shifted to the Americas and elsewhere. Wealth became concentrated among a small minority of the population as previous generations' fortunes of empire and industry morphed into inheritances.

This era peaked in the earliest years of the 20th century. From 1900 to the outbreak of World War I in 1914, the top 10% of the population of Britain and France owned 90% of assets and wealth, including land, financial assets and industry. The top 1% owned half. This was the Gilded Age, the Belle Époque. Wealth has always been highly concentrated. But now the discrepancies and the allegiances of the elites to networks over country were sharper and more visible.

And amid this world of plenty, British money stood supreme, commanding 69% of global capital, with investments that spanned the globe – but which largely avoided low-growth Britain, whose working classes struggled to unionise or otherwise improve their lot. At the heart of this world beat the Bank of England and its commitment to the international gold standard. The world was its oyster. And it all came crashing down.

THE RISE OF THE AMERICAN DOLLAR
World War I destroyed the 19th-century order, but London's primacy was already being challenged by New York and the American dollar.

The American experience with money was different from that of Britain and France. In 1840 Alexis de Tocqueville, that keenest of observers of early America, noted the lack of many large fortunes or hereditary

WASHINGTON

ONE DOLLAR

wealth. Much of this was owing to circumstance, such as America's abundance of agricultural land, but it was also about attitude. In Europe, the rich considered it crass to make money, and the poor knew it was a hopeless dream. But in America, making money was the national sport (albeit in the South, off the labour of black slaves). As a later president, Calvin Coolidge, put it, "The chief business of the American people is business."

It may seem bizarre, then, that Americans despised bankers. But in a country founded on the principles of the frontier and democracy, no issue loomed larger than money: what was currency, how much of it should exist and who should decide that? This question would dominate American politics from the republic's founding until World War I. The very fact that the broad population was consumed by arguments over money, and that such questions determined electoral outcomes, marked Americans as different.

From the get-go, a faction in the nascent republic, led by Alexander Hamilton, wanted to create a federal banking system that could benefit from the country's scale. Immediately after the Revolutionary War, in 1791 he cut a deal in which the various states allowed him,

as the country's treasury secretary, to securitise their war debts in the form of national bonds and set up a national bank.

This technocratic move ran into massive popular opposition, however, and not just from the owners of the many private banks now competing with Hamilton's national bank. Banks were the devil's tool of debt and bankruptcy, as any fool could tell you.

Hamilton's bank was chartered for just 20 years. The charter wasn't renewed, but Congress later approved another national bank in 1816. But neither held a monopoly on the issuance of paper notes.

This Second Bank of the United States held too few coin reserves and lent too aggressively, triggering recessions. Most state and private banks, on the other hand, were prudent with their lending and reserves. The national bank was ended by the election of a populist president, Andrew Jackson, a war hero from Tennessee who had little truck with fancy financiers from Philadelphia. Banking and note issuance went completely private, and by 1860 there were almost 3,000 banks operating in America.

But the heirs of Hamilton who wanted a federal system had not quit, and in the dark days of the American Civil War, they got their chance. Under President Abraham Lincoln, Congress (minus representatives of the rebelling South) passed laws authorising the printing of federal "greenback" notes, marking a return to fiat money. Congress also chartered federal banks.

America issued USD450m worth of greenbacks to finance the war. The notes depreciated heavily, but the government, buttressed by the growing industry of the North, would eventually prove good on its promises. It wouldn't be until 1879 that it let holders of greenbacks convert them into gold coins, but by that point, people had faith in the currency.

The Confederacy of the South also issued "yellowbacks". While in 1861, upon the start of the war, the South boasted more natural resources, it could not match the financial power of the North. Its wealth was based on land and slaves, not mechanised industry and credit. And most of the fighting took place in the South, devastating its infrastructure and capital. The Confederacy issued a whopping USD1 billion in yellowbacks, which lost nearly all their value.

This combination of overwhelming debt, physical destruction and evaporated capital cast much of the South into a century-long poverty – a harbinger of the destruction awaiting Europe 50 years later.

America wasn't done with its political battles over money, though. The country remained fixed on the tension between capitalism and democracy.

Republicans, backed by Northern industrialists and New York bankers, fought for a single gold standard backed by technical expertise. They became known as the goldbugs, and in 1873 they won the fight for the dollar to join the gold standard as run out of London.

Democrats, represented by their perennial presidential candidate William Jennings Bryan, argued for bimetallism. The gold standard was fine for Wall Street,

but the populists wanted unlimited printing of money based on silver to provide credit to hard-pressed farmers and workers. Their call to action was summed by candidate Bryan's speech in 1896, declaring, "You shall not crucify mankind upon a cross of gold."

But the goldbugs, buoyed by new gold discoveries in Alaska, won that battle too, and in 1900 Congress put America solely on the gold standard – without a central bank.

By then the American economy had eclipsed Britain's. But the dollar was a nonentity overseas, and American merchants had to negotiate international contracts in pounds sterling at prices guided by the Bank of England. The French franc and the German mark had also become important reserve currencies, but there was no demand among foreign central banks to hold greenbacks.

America's strength came from its farms and its industry, not from its financial infrastructure, which was primitive. Despite the pre-eminence of the greenback, state and private banks had control over how much to print. More banks kept opening, tens of thousands of them. They were constrained in that they couldn't open branches across state lines – and none had an international presence – but they were otherwise free to lend with little regulation.

Placing a gold standard on top of this freewheeling situation did not provide the hoped-for stability. And without a central bank, there was no lender of last resort. A panic in 1907 required the personal intervention of John Pierpoint Morgan, the nation's most influential banker. Putting such power in the hands of a private citizen was dangerous.

The combination of the need to modernise American finance and give the dollar its rightful place in the world led Congress to authorise the establishment of the Federal Reserve System in 1913. It was set up according to American views of decentralisation, comprising 12 governors representing different regions. But when a crisis came knocking – as it did immediately – the Fed would be tested and found wanting.

THE END OF THE GOLD STANDARD

World War I lasted from 1914 to 1918, with American intervention late in the action tipping the scales in favour of the Allies. A mechanised war of this duration and intensity led to unprecedented death and destruction. Amid the chaos, Lenin launched the Communist revolution in Russia and promptly began printing worthless money.

For Europe's wealthy 10%, the war was a shock. As soon as the shooting started, all the belligerents abandoned the gold standard. Global trade collapsed. Governments, desperate to finance the war, went on borrowing binges – even America had to issue war bonds. The Treaty of Versailles hobbled Germany and its allies with massive war reparations, while Britain and France were likewise saddled with debts to America.

The Bank of England, led by Montagu Norman and egged on by Winston Churchill, then chancellor of the exchequer, was determined to maintain the primacy of sterling. Britain returned to the gold standard in 1925. Central banks of the leading countries, including France and Germany, also had gold reserves, which they used to support the value of their currencies.

Before the war, the gold-dependent system seemed to work naturally. If France ran a trade deficit, its central bank would have to pay out gold to pay for the extra imports, causing domestic prices to fall and thereby making French goods more competitive. Then France would export more, and the central bank would receive gold from other countries.

But the era of the gold standard died with the war, even if no one grasped this. There would be no repeat of Napoleon's smooth return from fiat money to metallic coins: inflation had arrived.

The British had sold their foreign assets to pay for the war effort, returns on overseas investments were poor and the state began levying taxes to finance its debts. Perhaps if Norman had pegged sterling to a lower price, he could have boosted manufacturing and exports, but

In the US, banks were often viewed as the devil's tool of debt and bankruptcy

he was chasing the glory days of when the Bank and a strong pound were the centre of the world. In the end, the only thing the gold standard brought back was labour unrest.

Nor did sterling reclaim its role as the world's key reserve currency. During the 1920s, it competed against the greenback, which rapidly came to account for about half of all foreign-exchange reserves. But sterling regained pole position in the 1930s in the wake of the Great Depression, which destroyed confidence in Wall Street banks. The situation was worsened by an overly cautious Fed, which didn't understand the need for it to serve as the lender of last resort.

Germany and the states that emerged from the ashes of the Austro-Hungarian Empire struggled with reparations and recession. They printed money far beyond their meagre bullion reserves. Germany had been unified in the 1870s on the premise of an authoritarian state, but after the war it had attempted to operate under a parliamentary democracy. This nascent government was torn among political factions, including Communists and Hitler's Nazis. Whatever hopes the Weimar Republic had of survival were dashed by catastrophic hyperinflation due to the rampant printing of money.

The Wall Street crash of 1929 disrupted industry and banking everywhere. The gold standard, once a keeper of stability, had become a conduit for spreading chaos. Crippled by an uncompetitive manufacturing base, the Bank of England could not meet its foreign-exchange payments and abandoned the gold standard in 1931. By 1936, Germany, France and America had followed suit.

But what did it mean to leave the gold standard? The year 1936 was also when English economist John Maynard Keynes published "The General Theory of Employment, Interest and Money". Keynes regarded the gold standard as a "barbarous relic" that should be replaced by modern monetary management. Instead of passively waiting for economic shifts to occur, governments could increase or decrease demand via government spending. Whereas Marx had argued that capitalism caused depressions, Keynes showed that governments could use money as an instrument to tame capitalism's excesses.

His ideas were first put to the test in America, where President Franklin Delano Roosevelt relied on fiscal spending as part of his New Deal, a series of programmes, public work projects and financial reforms to escape the Great Depression. FDR took America off the gold standard so he could borrow – and spend – more freely.

But the gold standard would enjoy one last gasp. People were still wedded to the idea that money had to have some tie to metallic commodities to have value. In 1944, at Bretton Woods, New Hampshire, while the fighting still raged in Europe and the Pacific, America and its allies hammered out a new global monetary system with the greenback at its heart.

In this new arrangement, America promised to tie the dollar to gold, at USD35 per ounce. Other countries would peg their currencies to the dollar. The International Monetary Fund and the World Bank were founded to foster international trade, aid payments among members and ensure exchange-rate stability. The IMF was also meant to use its liquidity to help countries adjust their balance of payments if they faced an emergency redeeming currency for gold. At the same time, America launched the Marshall Plan, injecting cash into European countries to help them rebuild, modernise and cover foreign-exchange shortfalls. It was a time when governments, not markets, determined international capital flows.

For about 30 years, the Bretton Woods system underpinned high rates of growth and recovery in America, Europe and Japan. But by the 1960s the system was under strain. America was borrowing and spending heavily on domestic social programmes and funding its war in Vietnam. The increase in the money supply led to inflation. The dollar lost its value (in terms of gold), and the costs to the Treasury rose to meet

requests by other central banks (primarily France's) to convert dollars into gold.

Americans were wealthier than any other moment in human history, and they enjoyed spending. As Europe and Japan got back on their feet, their industries began selling more goods to America. Domestically, American largess was also fuelling inflation.

To American policymakers, eager to spend more on social programmes and the military, the gold standard had become a straitjacket. President Richard Nixon tried to get around this by implementing freezes on wages and prices and taxing imports, to no avail. Inflation continued to rage. So on August 15th 1971, he "closed the gold window", meaning he ordered the Federal Reserve to stop promising to sell gold to other central banks at a fixed price.

Now the dollar would trade freely against all other currencies. Other countries immediately followed. The world entered uncharted waters. The era of fiat money – the beginning of our generation's time – had begun.

Eager to spend more on social programs and the military, the gold standard became a straightjacket for President Nixon

THE ART OF CURRENCY

Banknotes and coins can be the playthings of artists, who are often keen to make statements about our consumer economy. The American dollar has been arranged as images – of skulls or red pickup trucks instead of presidential portraits. Dollars have been assembled to form sculptures. Portraits are made from banknotes.

When artists manipulate money this way, they are taking aim at finance, at governments, at society. Money has always been an abstraction, and artists are using it in the same way, but for a different end: to transact a message rather than to make a payment.

Taken too far, artists can find authorities lack a sense of humour or aesthetic appreciation. Take the case of Genpei Akasegawa. In 1963, he printed semblances of the JPY1,000 note, but just on one side, and then spent the next few months using them to make objects or burning them in performances. It was all in good fun, noticed only by Akasegawa's artist friends – and the Tokyo Metropolitan Police, who thought he had done too fine a job.

If the aim was to seed doubts about fiat money, the police did a better job than a young artist ever could. The resulting trial scrutinised fiat money rather than Akasegawa. The artist argued that his notes were obviously useless, but the court found him guilty and gave him a three-month suspended sentence.

The artist had said his works were representations of money, not money itself. But he had struck a nerve, because what is a representation of a representation? What lay at the core of the banknotes he was lampooning? Akasegawa responded to his sentencing with a new set of yen notes, created in 1967, which he called the Greater Japan Zero-yen Note. The zero-yen note was more than a prank: although it had explicitly no value, Akasegawa encouraged people to swap it for real money at a rate of JPY300 per fake note and start using his zero-yen as scrip. Once that happened, there would be no difference between his play money and the state's "real" money. By copying something that is itself valued only because of government fiat, the artist reveals what's really artificial.

11
FIAT

Following the end of the gold standard, the ascendancy of fiat money ushered in an era in which currencies took on a new life

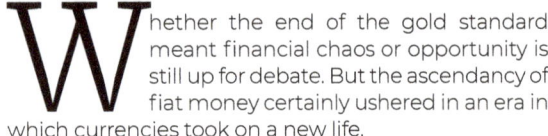

Whether the end of the gold standard meant financial chaos or opportunity is still up for debate. But the ascendancy of fiat money certainly ushered in an era in which currencies took on a new life.

In the Age of Discovery, great fortunes were made through trade, symbolised by European ships brimming with spices, slaves, silver and gold. In 18th-century Britain, industry became the driver of new wealth, on the back of steam engines and railroads. After 1945 the way to get rich was to run a big corporation, especially in America. After 1971, though, the fattest rewards came from finance. Technology had served to build other industries, from shipping to automobiles. With computers, which excel at processing information, tech was now put to work in the service of money.

Before World War I, only a handful of currencies traded internationally. Today, thanks to electronic markets, 180 national currencies can be traded almost instantly with just a few keystrokes or, more recently, swipes on a mobile phone.

The market for trading currencies – that is, the foreign-exchange market – now trades more than USD6.6 trillion a day says the Bank of International Settlements. That's more than 25 times the combined turnover of the world's stock markets. Even the American Treasury market, by far the world's largest bond market, only turned over approximately USD556 billion a day in 2018.

In other words, the market for money dwarfs that of securities, commodities such as oil and gold, electronics or automobiles. The second-largest market in the world is for financial derivatives: by April 2019, foreign-exchange (forex) derivatives experienced almost USD3.6 trillion of daily turnover, and interest-rate derivatives nearly USD3.7 trillion, according to the Bank of England.

One reason the forex market is so large is that it is liquid, and it is readily accessible to a broad array of investors, thanks to technology. Electronic brokers such as OANDA emerged in the 1990s, providing real-time information about prices among currency pairs. They also offered research and do-it-yourself trading capabilities to individuals and companies. In the process, the costs of trading began to fall, as brokers and other intermediaries could now process transactions in real time and at vast scale.

How, exactly, did we get here – and where are we headed?

The post-war period ushered in widespread changes to money, wealth and society. These came in roughly two phases: the three growth decades immediately following the war, and then financialisation that began with the end of the gold standard, which is now segueing into yet a third phase, the Age of Information.

LES TRENTES GLORIEUSES

The French have a name for what happened in developed countries following the Second World War: Les Trentes Glorieuses (the glorious 30 years). They refer to an incredible economic renaissance that benefited the entire populations of Western Europe and Japan as they strove to achieve prosperity like America's.

From the European perspective, this period began with the Marshall Plan, was extended by the dirigisme (active economic direction) of the state, and ended with an oil price shock in the early 1970s.

Along with growth came inflation, which destroys the value of money. But during Les Trentes Glorieuses, economic growth was high enough that inflation felt only moderate. And there were other reasons the debasement of currency felt tolerable.

The wars and the Great Depression had cost the European colonial powers and Japan their empires, depriving the rentiers of the income streams to which they had grown accustomed. Income taxes were levied in developed countries to pay for the war, and then to fund government programmes in response to

Following World War II, many parts of the world experienced an economic renaissance

economic misery. The landed aristocracies of Europe and Japan, and to an extent the gilded barons of America, had their wealth stripped from them.

At the same time, government expanded in new ways. Under President Franklin Delano Roosevelt, America took active measures to combat recession and restore the labour market. His New Deal program of legislation included funding for pensions, unemployment and health care. It created a bureaucracy to administrate grandiose infrastructure programmes and to regulate financial markets.

European governments embraced socialism after the war, whether in Clement Attlee's Britain or Charles de Gaulle's France, or among the Christian-democratic parties of Germany and Italy. They further extended the reach of the state to promote welfare to a citizenry that, exhausted by war and economic collapse, demanded support.

Universal state welfare dates to Otto von Bismarck, the dynamic first chancellor of a unified Germany. During the 1880s he initiated the world's first state insurance programmes by a central government for workers. He did so to tie their loyalties to the state and to head off more liberal or socialist forces urging workers to campaign for workplace protections or other measures that would disrupt industry. Japan pursued similar policies that, in the 1930s, morphed into cradle-to-grave welfare designed to militarise the entire population.

Post-war democratic politicians, on the other hand, generated legitimacy by financing health, education, housing and workplace safety laws. As a result, America, Europe and Japan created the modern middle class. Whereas before the wars, Europe's top 10% controlled 90% of the wealth, now the middle classes could own a home and claim up to one-third of national wealth.

The financial world during this period was constrained. The only big speculative market was the stock exchange. Private-sector debt was modest: in 1950, it represented about 50% of national income throughout the developed world. That's because banks were constrained in their ability to create credit. One piece of New-Deal legislation, the Glass-Steagall Act, barred deposit-taking banks from undertaking risky activities. Another New Deal measure called Regulation Q limited the amount of interest that banks could charge on deposits with chequing accounts and required them to hold high levels of reserve capital (meaning the money could not be lent out).

Beyond America, the IMF helped maintain stability and the gold standard, and leading currencies barely moved in relation to one another. Bretton Woods had fixed other currencies such as sterling to the dollar to avoid the sort of competitive devaluations that had plagued the world economy during the Great Depression. Such pegs ensured ease of foreign trade because there was no currency risk, but they put a crimp on the free movement of capital across borders.

Even before Nixon ended the gold standard, the era was inevitably winding down. Regulation Q's limits on banking applied only to America. They didn't apply to the deposits of Americans held with foreign banks overseas – even if those funds were then lent back to American banks. In the 1960s, therefore, European banks in the City of London began doing just that, offering American depositors favourable interest rates while charging American banks a fee to reroute money back to them. American banks with branches in London could ramp up lending based on American deposits without having to count the money towards their capital charges.

Thus was born what became known as the Eurodollar market, which ushered in arbitrage. Arbitrage was originally how financiers such as Nathan Rothschild found the best price for a given foreign-exchange trade. Now it also described how global financial institutions played off the regulations of different countries to generate revenues. During the period in which the world's currencies traded in tandem, the Eurodollar market remained modest. But when currencies all floated, this ushered in a new world of massive capital flows across markets. Currencies proved volatile, which encouraged the rise of forex traders, while the opportunity of arbitrage set off a competition among countries for attracting capital. Dirigisme gave way to laissez-faire capitalism.

FUTURES AND NEW WAYS TO CREATE MONEY

The 1970s was that most fascinating of periods: a transitory moment in which one era dies and another is born. This was the decade in which the building blocks of our techno-capitalism were laid, beginning with Nixon's floating of currencies. Freeing money led to vast new opportunities in international trade and triggered an explosion of bank credit creation that continues today. But the vast majority of this new money operates outside of classic regulation, in a grey zone called shadow banking – and therefore represents a rupture with the "great monetary settlement" underpinning the creation of the Bank of England.

That fateful year, 1971, saw the founding of the world's first electronic stock market, which is now known as the Nasdaq. It began as a quotation system, using computers to provide more accurate pricing of stocks that traded "over the counter", that is, not on a traditional bourse such as the New York Stock Exchange. The technology had been developed by Bernie Madoff, a marketmaker who made bids and offers on OTC stocks. His technology turned a niche, opaque market into one that was transparent and liquid, and the Nasdaq went on to become the second-largest exchange in America, known especially for listing technology companies.

One year later, in 1972, Leo Melamed introduced financial futures contracts at the Chicago Mercantile Exchange. These instruments allowed people to hedge exposures or take speculative bets without owning the underlying assets. Financial futures, along with electronic broking and the rise of cross-border capital flows, led to a massive expansion in financial activity.

Futures are derivatives that trade on an exchange. Derivatives are important, if misunderstood, financial tools. Today they come in for plenty of criticism because the market is big, opaque and largely unregulated. But their origins date further back than 1972. Indeed, it's worth a quick detour to understand how they got their start, to demonstrate that these tools transcend stereotypes about Anglo-American free-market capitalism.

The records written in clay by ancient Mesopotamians prove people have been using derivatives for a very long time. These earliest civilisations developed populations too large to feed, so food had to be imported, particularly given that Sumer and other cities were not built on cereal-producing land. Ensuring reliability of food supplies at predictable prices was critical.

Hammurabi's Code approved the sale of goods for a certain price to be delivered on a certain date. Babylonian writing evolved to assign such contracts, and Hammurabi promised that breakers of promises would be penalised by death.

It's likely that ziggurats, the mighty temples of ancient Mesopotamia, served as commercial hubs for trading and storing grain, just as Buddhist monasteries would 2,000 years later. Sumer's priests and royal scribes would have set rules of volume and quality for the trading of cereals. The written evidence suggests Sumerians used what we now call forward contracts for bilateral sales and purchases. It is possible, though unknown, that they made such contracts tradable, which would have allowed brokers to step in and facilitate speculation around them.

Hammurabi's legal system endured until Alexander the Great conquered Mesopotamia and replaced it with a Greek, coin-based economy. The Greeks and especially the Romans, with their advanced legal systems, possessed the ingredients for derivatives. But such activities were limited due to the preference for using coins; bilateral agreements existed, but nothing like a market. The new Christian and Islamic faiths condemned derivatives as gambling and usury, restrictions that not even the creative bankers of Italy could sidestep.

It was not until the emergence of capitalism in the Netherlands that forward contracts began to circulate in northern Europe, in Antwerp, Amsterdam, Hamburg, Danzig and London. By the 1530s, bilateral forwards were being traded on foreign exchange, enabling merchants to protect their long-distance commerce from the fluctuations of currencies against the guilder – or to simply take a punt. These were the cities that saw the arrival of joint-stock companies and stock markets, and soon the Dutch and British could "write" forwards and options on anything from English East India Company stock to tulip bulbs.

But for the first futures market, the story shifts to 17th-century Japan. Monetary history in East Asia tends to focus on China, but its innovative period had come to an end and its governments tried to strictly regulate commerce and foreign trade. China had credit institutions, but a hobbled securities market limited the impact of its banks. The same was true in neighbouring countries that drew inspiration from Chinese culture. But something in Japan changed.

THE DOJIMA RICE EXCHANGE

Around 1600, after 100 years of civil war and chaos, the shogun Ieyasu Tokugawa established a dynasty that imposed peace and stability across the archipelago, which in turn sparked a renewal of commerce and urbanisation. Japan remained feudal with peasants tied to the land, but it also had a lively market economy in cities such as Osaka and Edo (Tokyo).

Japan also operated under three types of currency: gold coins denominated in ryo (the precursor to the yen), silver coins and copper coins. But given constant shortages of gold and silver, rice served as a substitute currency. Indeed, government budgets and lords' local taxes were calculated in terms of rice, to be converted into metallic money at town markets. Most of the rice was warehoused in Osaka.

The story goes as follows: Chozaemon, a rice merchant from Nagoya, journeys to Edo. Along the way he meets a traveller from Sendai, way up north. They strike a deal to share information about whether the rice harvest in their respective regions is doing well or not.

Five years later they meet again, and the man from Sendai says the northern harvest looks bleak, so prices are going to rise. Chozaemon knows the south, on the other hand, is poised to enjoy a bumper crop. He begins hoarding southern rice orders. Friends ask him to do the same, purchasing 500 ryo of rice on their behalf. Chozaemon has nowhere to store all of this rice. So he cuts a deal: friends can pay him 60 ryo up front, and when he sells the rice the next year, they can pay the rest of the 440 ryo and he will give them the profits, minus a small fee. But if he's wrong about prices going up – if they actually fall, and all of that rice they bought for 500 ryo sells at a loss – then he still keeps the 60 ryo.

This is how hedging works. The middleman earns a premium for offering a sophisticated form of insurance or speculative gain. A derivative is something that derives its value based on the performance of something else. An Osaka rice forward's value depends on the price of rice.

Soon feudal lords muscled in, issuing rice receipts that entitled the bearer to prearranged amounts of rice from their warehouses in Osaka. The premiums ensured them a steady stream of income.

But unlike tulips or company stock, rice in Japan was also a currency. These receipts became like currencies themselves, and their value fluctuated apart from that of the actual rice. Warehouses issued bills that merchants and lords traded as forms of credit, and lords soon began writing "empty" rice bills that were backed by only a fraction of the notional amount on the contract.

At first this activity took place in private merchants' houses, but in 1697 the Osaka city government moved everything to a new site, the Dojima Rice Exchange.

Feudal lords muscled in on the Dojima
Rice Exchange, which was the world's first
commodity futures exchange

Paving the way for the futures market, Hammurabi's Code approved the sale of goods for an agreed price to be delivered on a certain date

Making this possible was another Dojima innovation: the "book" transaction system in which all trades were recorded in a single ledger. A clearing-house system emerged out of the money-changing business. A clearing house served as the counterparty to both sides of the trade, so buyers and sellers transacted with it instead of directly with one another. With the liquidity of scale and informed by its book, the clearing house guaranteed trades and ensured daily settlement. This relieved merchants of the need to have the full amount of rice or coins on hand. Instead they held collateral, rice or ryo, with the clearing house.

A futures exchange is a place to trade standardised forward contracts and Dojima was the first place where this occurred, thanks to standardisation created by the clearing house and the need to manage multiple currencies. (It also helped that Japan had no religious qualms about charging interest.)

At first the government was hands-off, but then it blamed Dojima for a rise in rice prices and banned futures trading. This curtailed liquidity, however, and rice prices crashed. This was a problem given that samurai generals were paid in rice. In 1730, the shogun reauthorised futures trading and the market flourished. This would continue until the eve of the Second World War.

For 300 years the Japanese traded financial futures, bringing predictability and liquidity to the rice market in a largely self-regulated environment. Futures also transformed the nature of commerce, thanks to social rules that evolved at Dojima and ensured ostracism for deal-breakers. This allowed merchants to trade with strangers instead of having to rely on kinship networks, even for highly risky and speculative investments.

THE GREAT MODERATION

Tokugawa Japan is about as far away culturally, socially and economically from 1970s America as can be imagined. Yet it was feudal Osaka and capitalist Chicago that both created financial futures exchanges, in other words, sophisticated currency-like contracts connected to underlying assets. They both allowed for a vast expansion of financial instruments to be traded. But whereas Dojima was limited to rice in an isolated economy, the Chicago Mercantile Exchange pioneered financial derivatives in a world of floating currencies and electronic trading.

The post-1971 explosion in financial instruments – currencies, stocks, bonds, derivatives – changed both the scope and the nature of the modern finance industry. Before, finance was based on confidence in the other party: *credere* (to believe, to credit). Financial intermediaries were usually agents; they worked for a buyer or a seller, whether in feudal Japan, Victorian London or wild-west America. Now, however, the action shifted to trading as financial institutions worked for their own books, even if that created a conflict of interest between serving clients and serving the firm.

This new kind of finance would change the world in a different sector, however. In 1977, Lew Ranieri, working at the newly established mortgage desk of Salomon Brothers in New York, invented the mortgage-backed security.

Mortgages are bank loans to homebuyers. In America, politicians catered to middle-class voters with the "American dream" of home ownership. New Deal institutions were designed to buy mortgages from local banks, to encourage them to extend home loans. And banks liked mortgages because in the event of default, they could claim the house as collateral.

Ranieri's innovation was to "securitise" mortgages by bundling a commercial bank's home loans into a security that investors could purchase or trade. This was taking the original insight of Renaissance Italian bankers – recording a new asset and liability on its ledger created instant purchasing power – and industrialising it. Securitisation greatly expanded the amount of capital that was now available for mortgages, making it cheaper for more middle- and lower-income families to buy a house. Securitisation also supported economic dynamism: in America, most start-up businesses rely on the owner's house as a key source of funding.

Securitisation did something else, though: it eroded the commercial bank's incentive to study borrower risk. As Wall Street investment banks began buying up pools of loans, local lenders could simply transfer the risk of default to New York. Wall Street bankers, on the other hand, used computers to assess broader trends without worrying about the quality of individual loans. They just packaged these into bond-like instruments and sold them to someone else, often to European banks and pension funds, which had even less of a clue about the end borrower.

Securitisation is just the most visible evidence that the machinery for creating money had changed. The original fractional-reserve banking, in which deposits are turned into loans, become securitised, with "deposits" and "loans" structured as contracts that banks buy and sell.

What this means is that banks are creating credit out of nothing, and this is our money supply – accounting for up to 97% of money worldwide. This private debt includes consumer debt (especially mortgages, along with credit-card debt, student loans, automobile loans and unsecured loans) and business debt for big companies – but this money is being structured as securities for the financial system, with only a small percentage being lent out directly to businesses. Money created for productive uses is healthy and

While securitisation supported economic dynamism, it also eroded the incentive for banks to study borrower risk

sustainable, but money created for investing in assets, particularly real estate, creates inflation and financial bubbles.

But the dangers of securitisation – and the broader changes in finance – would not be apparent for a while. The political mood in America and Britain shifted to free-market liberalism, based on assumptions that markets were perfectly efficient and that governments were impediments to economic development.

Margaret Thatcher and Ronald Reagan, both free-market conservatives, were totems of this era in the 1980s, but the drive to deregulate was also pursued by their left-wing successors in the 1990s. Regulatory limits were scrapped, allowing banks to combine retail deposits with high-risk investment banking and trading. Central banks pulled back from active supervision of commercial lenders. The tearing up of the "great monetary settlement", in which sovereigns allowed private money creation so long as it was regulated, was an act committed by both commercial banks and governments.

This had implications far beyond the financial-services industry. In the corporate world, led by figures such as Jack Welch, chief executive of General Electric, the mantra was "shareholder value" and corporate leaders were rewarded with stock options. To shareholders, companies had become disembodied blips on their computer screens, usually bundled in the form of indexed products. Ownership became detached from the workers, customers and suppliers of businesses. Capital was allocated in ways that boosted share prices, often without regard for a company's long-term growth.

Banks grew very large and profitable. Boutique partnerships became listed investment banks, beginning with Lehman Brothers in 1994. American investment banks globalised and European banks tried to remake themselves in the American image. Their biggest moneymaking units were in fixed-income, currency and commodity trading, and the most lucrative part of the business was securitisation. Trading itself became increasingly computerised, led

by "quants" with PhDs in physics or engineering who sliced securitised loans into ever-riskier tranches with ever-decreasing attention to credit risk.

These developments occurred in a global environment of free trade, democracy and economic liberalism, underpinned by a Pax Americana that enabled East Asia and Europe to prosper. The collapse of Communism in 1989-1991 gave liberalism further impetus and brought Eastern Europe into the capitalist fold. Even China, while sticking to authoritarian rule, embarked on a bold reform movement under Deng Xiaoping.

This was the Great Moderation, another kind of Les Trentes Glorieuses. It was a time of both exhilarating stability and progress, but also one of unprecedented and increasing turbulence. But to Americans and Europeans, financial crises at home were ephemeral, while the real chaos stirred in faraway places such as Latin America, Russia and East Asia.

Indeed, it was Japan that suffered the mother of all stock bubbles. Japanese banks, under government guidance, had channelled the country's excessive reserves from exports into industry. In the 1980s, though, they switched to investing in real estate and the stock market. This credit fuelled boom led to a single square mile of Tokyo land being valued more than the entire property market of California, an apocryphal but not outlandish story. The property and stock markets crashed in 1988, and 30 years later, the Tokyo Stock Exchange's indices still haven't recovered more than about half their peak value.

Of course, bubbles are a regular feature of capitalism. Holland, the first capitalist society, had its fling with tulips. London had its South Sea Company mishap, concurrent with the devastating Mississippi Company disaster in Paris. And so on, all the way to the 1929 Wall Street crash that ushered in the Great Depression. It seemed, however, that the credo of free markets had now introduced a new, durable stability with America at its heart. A financial crisis, everyone agreed, could never happen there.

WOMEN ON BANKNOTES

Women appeared on the earliest banknotes printed in Europe. When the Bank of England printed its first notes in 1694, they showed a representation of Britannia, a feminine symbol of Great Britain. But, as with women monarchs putting their images on coins, Britannia is decked out in armour. France's Queen Marianne followed suit, presented in the style of a Roman goddess.

America, Austria, Sweden and other countries followed the same style, presenting themselves as tough but civilised. The concept endured through the 20th century: in 1960, Communist China issued banknotes portraying peasant women driving tractors.

But while banknotes throughout history frequently portrayed men – monarchs, scientists, financiers, adventurers – it wasn't until quite late in the 19th century that the first living women were presented as suitable national symbols. Queen Victoria was first presented on notes, not in Britain, but in Canada and Australia, in 1860. Other countries, such as Russia and Egypt, began issuing notes showing historical queens.

It wasn't until 1960 that the Bank of England printed its first notes portraying the living monarch, Queen Elizabeth II. This shift away from more abstract images of nationhood was less a campaign for women's representation and more an assertion of the power of the state in the era of fiat money.

The first historical woman portrayed on pound notes was Florence Nightingale, who aided wounded soldiers during the 19th century Crimean War but wasn't recognised until she appeared on a GBP10 note in 1975.

America didn't put a woman on its national currency until the 1880s and 1890s, when the US Mint issued silver certificates featuring Martha Washington. The 1860s briefly portrayed Pocahontas on the back of the USD20 note.

But that was the last time a woman appeared on American notes. Nor have they featured much on coins: the Mint issued a commemorative coin in 1893 of Spain's Queen Isabella, marking four centuries since she had sponsored Columbus's voyage. But no actual American was again portrayed until the Susan B. Anthony coin was struck in 1979 to recognise the suffragette.

The Obama administration had planned to revise the USD20 note, replacing the slave-owning, anti-bank President Andrew Jackson with Harriet Tubman, the celebrated escapee who operated the Underground Railroad. The Trump administration, which seems to have a soft spot for white slave-owning patriarchs, has put those plans on hold.

America is not alone in this embarrassing oversight. Most countries' paper money has no portrayals of women. A notable exception is Australia: all of its notes show a prominent man on one side and a famous woman on the other – or perhaps it's the other way around.

12
CRISES

In 2008, the Global
Financial Crisis
devastated stock
markets, bringing the
entire financial system
to its knees

The Great Moderation of 1981 to 2007 was a mirage, masking a huge build-up of private-sector credit that was expressed in a booming bond market, especially in securitised mortgages. American mortgages grew from 2001 to 2007, from USD5 trillion to USD10 trillion, a massive increase in runaway lending. Total US private-sector debt rose from 50% of GDP in 1945 to 160% in 2007. The flip side of creating a liability is the creation of an asset, in this case, a bond. Investment banks were creating vast numbers of bonds, which in turn fostered a market for interest-rate derivatives. These emerged from zero in 1980 to USD400 trillion of notional outstanding in 2007. Most of this growth in financial instruments was affiliated with credit securitisation.

Credit booms spark economic growth, which is fine if the money is repaid. But when credit is created in the form of debts that can't be repaid, the system crashes and everyone gets hurt. This is how harmful booms and busts always work: credit becomes too readily available, and then a change in economic conditions causes it to immediately dry up.

In the US, the erosion of credit analysis in home loans manifested itself in the 2008 global financial crisis (GFC). It felled securitisation packagers such as Lehman Brothers, devastated stock markets and brought the entire financial system to its knees. (As liquidity dries up, crashes also tend to unveil fraudsters, one of whom turned out to be Bernie Madoff.)

Debt-related crises are nothing new. In ancient Mesopotamia, the arrival of a new king was often accompanied by the cancellation of debts as a way of restarting the system. The Israelites created the Jubilee (year of release); every 49 years, debts were forgiven, properties returned and slaves freed. In modern times, there are no convenient ways for kings to reset the books. Instead, from the Latin American crisis of overborrowing from oil-rich countries, to the Mexican "tequila" crisis, the Russian default and the Asian financial crisis of the 1990s, countries borrowed too much (usually in dollars)

and suddenly found no one would roll over the debt into another round of financing.

The GFC was not a crisis of emerging markets. It emanated from the heart of global capitalism. The severity of the credit boom and bust was such that Washington threw out the capitalist rulebook. The US and UK response was to socialise the losses of the banking sector – making this a jubilee for bankers but not for homeowners or savers.

The Federal Reserve, mindful of its role as lender of last resort, stepped in by buying lots and lots of mortgage securities and slashing interest rates. It did so by essentially printing money, by creating assets and liabilities on its balance sheet. The assets were used to buy mortgages, but the liabilities remained on the Fed's books. The idea behind this programme, called quantitative easing, was to inject liquidity into the banking system so that banks would resume lending. It worked to the extent that the world avoided a catastrophe reminiscent of the Great Depression. Nonetheless quantitative easing coupled with fiscal bailouts represented a huge rescue of the private money-creating financial system.

Quantitative easing staved off mass bank collapses, but it didn't address the underlying causes of the crash. American and European commercial banks failed to rev up their credit machines, instead channelling their central bank-created balances to investments in financial assets, such as stocks and real estate, which enjoyed heady recoveries. Corporate bosses engaged in share buybacks but didn't invest in job-creating productivity. The real economy stagnated and jobs were lost, particularly in manufacturing.

The fiat financial system had come to this: private banks created money and when they got into trouble, central banks bailed them out. The system was broken. The irony is that the US dollar, the symbol and dominant currency in this fiat world, did not collapse. On the contrary, global investors sought the safety of US Treasuries instead of fleeing the epicentre of the crisis.

Mindful of its role as lender of last resort, the Federal Reserve stepped in to save the banks

The dollar has remained strong relative to other fiat currencies. That was even the case after the Republican Party risked a US sovereign default in a reckless political gamble against the Democratic presidency of Barack Obama. What does that tell us about the nature of money in this world of unfettered fiat?

CURRENCY CRISES

Because the money markets are the largest and most liquid in the world, currencies become expressions of investor fear or confidence in the countries they represent. When money flows in and out of a country, there is an underlying asset involved – a deposit, a security, real estate – that is denominated in the local currency. Currency pairs are zero-sum reflections of these underlying flows. If the value of the dollar versus the pound goes up, then the value of the pound versus the dollar must go down by the same degree.

But currencies are not purely financial instruments. The value of a country's exchange rate is also linked to its monetary supply and its economic growth. Economists have struggled to solve what they call the trilemma, or the "impossible trinity". It is impossible, says the trilemma, for a country to enjoy an independent monetary policy, free capital flows and a free rate of foreign exchange. A government must accept constraints somewhere in how it manages its economy.

This trilemma didn't matter so much during Les Trentes Glorieuses, when foreign exchange rates were tightly managed and international capital flows were constrained. Since the 1970s, this has no longer been the case. Most countries compete for foreign capital to invest in their industries and assets. Some do so by tying their currency or their monetary policy to a stronger entity – in other words, by making the trilemma work in their favour.

These artificial arrangements work well for a time, but inevitably conditions change. The impact can be very damaging, such as with Argentina's various ill-fated attempts to peg its peso to the US dollar. But Argentina is a small, marginal market. What happens when currency swings impact significant leading economies?

The impact is considerable. Take the case of Britain, which in the 1980s tried various means to manage the pound against a basket of European currencies, especially the Deutsche (West German) mark.

In 1992 investors such as hedge-fund manager George Soros realised sterling had been incorrectly valued against the Deutsche mark. Remember Britain's attempt to return to the gold standard after the First World War? Its policymakers have a track record of overconfidence in their economy's ability to match continental Europe's. Upon such delusions the vultures of the capital markets thrive.

In this case, Soros knew that to keep sterling from falling below its politically agreed upon range against the Deutsche mark, the Bank of England would have to keep raising interest rates. Soros made a spectacular bet by shorting the pound over the summer of 1992, leading to a high-stakes bluffing game. Who would blink first? The Bank of England, pressured to keep raising interest rates at the risk of causing a recession at home? Or Soros, who had to fund what eventually grew to a USD10 billion short position?

In September, the Old Lady of Threadneedle Street surrendered and devalued the pound. The currency dropped like a rock against the Deutsche mark and the dollar, and Soros reputedly pocketed a cool USD1 billion in profits.

The bet against sterling had an enormous impact on Britain's economy. The sting from the fracas was one reason the UK would refuse to join the euro upon its creation seven years later. But in other respects, the fallout was limited. This was a contest between insiders. Currency markets were not yet traded electronically, so there was no retail speculator. Only global banks, large corporate treasuries and big investment firms could play in this arena.

The British takeaway was to respect the power of free markets and keep sterling out of future artificial arrangements. Continental Europeans, however, drew a different lesson – informal monetary arrangements were too arbitrary. What was needed was a full-blown monetary union: otherwise the EU's dream of free movement of capital, goods, labour and services would founder upon the frictions of managing more than two dozen currencies. A monetary union would also require member states to harmonise their fiscal policies, plus a European central bank to coordinate members' domestic banking systems.

The creation of the euro, merging the currencies of 19 of the 28 members of the European Union, was a bold experiment in creating a monetary union. The project has always been political at its heart, as a means of binding Europe's fragmented nations into a bloc that could compete on the scale of the US, Russia and China.

In some respects, the euro has been a massive success. From the outset, it has been the second most liquid and traded currency in the world, after the US dollar. Much of this is due to the brave German decision to allow its Deutsche mark and the highly regarded Bundesbank to be subsumed into the greater European project.

In the wake of the global financial crisis of 2008, however, the euro came under terrible pressure. Although the GFC originated in US securitised real estate, European banks were among the biggest buyers of this toxic debt. They counted on it to fund their daily operations because they lacked the scale to amass enough retail deposits.

French, German, Dutch and British banks then went on to lend profligately to poorer eurozone borrowers in places such as Greece and Spain. These borrowers were taking advantage of low eurozone interest rates (thank you, Germany), but their tatty finances meant they couldn't repay their loans. This became clear when the Greek government fessed up to having cooked its fiscal books. Suddenly the very idea of the euro was in doubt.

As the GFC turned into a eurozone crisis, global investors doubled down on their quest for safe havens – assets most likely to preserve their value. The US bond market remains the biggest such safe haven, largely because it is the only financial market in the world that can accommodate almost unlimited capital inflows. But investors had reasons to be concerned about America's fiscal imprudence and political foolhardiness. Besides, a simple rule of investing (if not of life) is "Don't put all of your eggs in one basket." With the euro's very existence now in question, investors were desperate to find more baskets.

There are only a handful of safe havens, including the Japanese yen, thanks to Tokyo's huge government debt issuance. But to stave off recession, the Bank of Japan embarked on another round of quantitative easing. Combined with rock-bottom interest rates (in place in Japan since the 2000s as a reaction to the 1989 stock-market crash), the yen was not very attractive either.

This left Switzerland as the favourite safe haven.

Since the 1970s, the Swiss National Bank (SNB) has pursued an aggressive policy of managing the Swiss franc. Central banks of large economies focus their attention on keeping domestic inflation low and stable, using tools such as the interest they pay commercial banks on the reserves held at the central bank. But Switzerland, although rich and stable, is not a large economy. Since the 1970s, the SNB has pursued an active interventionist policy to keep the "Swissie" stable against European currencies. It often intervenes in Swiss assets that trade in London, the largest market for international debt, in order to influence interest rates on Swiss debt. Over time, the SNB became trusted by markets to maintain a strong and stable franc.

The Swiss National Bank crisis was the craziest event in currency markets in the fiat era

And in the 2010s, the franc became a favoured haven against the GFC, doubts about the euro, the prospect of an unruly Greek expulsion from the eurozone and tumbling yields in euro-denominated debt as countries such as Germany slashed interest rates.

But too much investor love was problematic for the SNB. Switzerland's economy depends on exports (think pharmaceuticals and luxury watches). Capital fleeing into Swiss assets sent the Swissie skyrocketing, hurting exporters and threatening deflation (because the price of imports kept falling).

Like other central banks, the SNB had been frantically expanding its own balance sheet, but not to buy Swiss francs. Instead, it was buying euros to shift the dynamics of supply and demand. Markets ignored it, so in 2011 the SNB did something drastic. It announced it would peg the value of the Swiss franc to the euro at CFH/EUR1.20 (that's 1.20 francs per euro). By making such a dramatic policy announcement, the SNB was telling the markets it was serious about capping the value of the Swissie.

All this did, however, was saddle the SNB with a growing pile of ever-depreciating euros. By 2014, its euro reserves amounted to 70% of Swiss GDP – an absurd level. Meanwhile, many Swiss citizens read this as simply a lot of money-printing that would (they assumed) tip the country into hyperinflation. The eurozone's mess was only getting worse, so foreign capital just kept pouring in. The SNB realised if it kept the peg, it would have to keep creating money to buy yet more euros.

The European Central Bank muddled through its crisis when its governor, Mario Draghi, promised to "do what it takes" to save the euro and unleashed his asset-purchasing programme. But small countries can't always "do what it takes". The SNB, by making a promise it couldn't keep, got into real trouble.

In January 2015 the SNB threw in the towel. The peg was scrapped. To manage the blow, it then slashed Swiss interest rates to negative 0.75%. If investors wanted to hold Swiss bank deposits, they'd have to pay the Swiss bank for the privilege. Another absurdity.

In 1992, when the British pound tumbled out of its managed peg with the Deutsche mark, the impact in financial markets was short-lived. But the SNB's surrender occurred in a different era, one in which electronic brokers had made currency trading available to households around the world. It also took place in an environment in which commercial banks' funding was elaborately connected to vast, intraday, electronic interbank trades.

This activity came to a grinding halt one January morning in 2015. Caught without warning, banks and their investors panicked. The Swiss franc dropped by 30% against the euro and 25% against the dollar in a matter of minutes. For nearly an hour there was no liquidity, meaning no one could exit their Swiss franc positions. Currency brokers typically make positions with leverage. Their leverage levels are quite modest compared to what happens in other markets, but even so, being stuck for this long in an electronic marketplace meant destruction. Several brokers went bankrupt, and major commercial banks including Citi, Barclays and Deutsche Bank lost hundreds of millions of dollars. And the Swiss stock market collapsed.

This was the craziest, most dangerous event in currency markets in the fiat era. Central banks are supposed to be slow and predictable, but the SNB found itself in an impossible situation, so it broke its commitment. Aside from those who lost their businesses, the SNB is the biggest loser of the affair. It sacrificed investor trust, but is still saddled with vast euro holdings, is stuck with negative interest rates (badly hurting ordinary Swiss citizens with money in the bank) and is less able to influence interest rates on debt traded through the London interbank market. Any attempt to normalise the situation will just invite another wave of foreign capital.

The lesson is sobering: in our world of fiat money, even solid, trusted authorities often find themselves unable to control their money. The best they can do is cling by their fingernails. This is going to be true of any currency in a managed situation.

The Hong Kong dollar, for example, has been successfully pegged to the greenback since 1983 at HKD7.80 per US dollar. This arrangement is widely regarded as a success. It has been durable, the Hong Kong Monetary Authority successfully defended against a hedge-fund attack in 1997-98, and the city is a trusted global financial centre.

Hong Kong is not a safe haven, however. It remains tied to the greenback by means of its own financial firepower. Since the GFC, the macroeconomic conditions have made a nonsense of the peg. Hong Kong's economy is intimately connected to that of mainland China. China experienced terrific growth, although it is increasingly fuelled by debt. At the same time, though, Hong Kong mirrored America's ultra-low interest rates. The combination has inflated asset prices in the city, notably in real estate.

The extremes of capitalist inequality are on stark display, with a handful of tycoon property owners becoming unimaginably rich while few ordinary people can afford to buy a flat. This provided the background music to mass street protests in 2014 and 2019. China's own economy is now slowing, notably in the face of a trade war sparked by the US. The situation has hedge funds wondering just how much firepower the Hong Kong authorities can muster should market vultures have another go at shorting the local stock market.

THE DOLLAR AND ITS CHALLENGERS

And what of the US dollar? In a world awash with money, the "almighty dollar" has retained and even extended its supreme position. The dollar's standing recalls sterling's enduring power even after Britain had ceded economic leadership to America and Germany. The dollar and dollar-denominated assets are the world's deepest, most liquid instruments, and the Fed

has ably served the world as the lender of last resort. Even the forex market is really a dollar market: today around 88% of all foreign-exchange trades involve the dollar on one side of the trade, even if neither party is American nor is trading US assets. This is unprecedented. Even sterling always shared reserve status with the French franc, the German mark and later the greenback.

How sustainable is dollar leadership? History shows there's no rule that only one currency can serve as the reserve. When sterling was the paramount currency, it still competed against the French franc and the Deutsche mark. And when the dollar challenged sterling for leadership, they existed in a pas de deux; without wars and depressions, sterling could have maintained primacy for a long time. So there is no law about how long the monetary system can be organised around a particular currency, or even if a hegemon is required.

But history also shows that no regime is permanent, and today's apparent dollar dominance could be as intangible as sterling's on the eve of 1914.

The euro and the Chinese yuan are possible alternatives, while other major economies such as those of India or Brazil could one day see their currencies grow in importance. Let's look at the euro first.

Greece's announcement that it could not repay its debts in 2009 sparked a eurozone crisis. More assets flowed to the US for safety, while the euro faced the possibility of annihilation.

To date, the euro has survived, with France and Germany keen to maintain it as a symbol of European unity. In terms of international debt markets, many bonds are denominated in euros, far more than in any currency other than the dollar. But it remains a distant number two in currency markets.

To promote the euro as a serious reserve currency, the eurozone will require more than just better fiscal

In today's forex market, the Chinese yuan has emerged as a serious contender to the greenback

Recently, Beijing has been aggressively pursuing its Belt and Road Initiative

coordination among member governments. It needs a full capital-markets union and a single sovereign asset, i.e. a eurobond. The example of the dollar overtaking sterling in the 1920s teaches that a reserve currency must be perceived by commercial and central banks as safe and liquid. Europe's political and banking structure today cannot ensure this because any change must start with a German agreement to transfer capital to weaker economies in times of need – an idea the German taxpayer has so far rejected.

The US experience suggests things could change. In 1913 America had a currency capable of playing a global role, but lacked the financial infrastructure to support this. But then it rolled out several reforms and launched the Federal Reserve, and within a few years the dollar had become a rival of the pound.

But for now, Europe will not enact the necessary reforms. Countries that fear being fleeced by their neighbours, such as Germany, will delay. Countries chafing against fiscal constraints within the eurozone, such as Italy, could resort to toying with parallel currencies, cryptocurrencies or direct transfers from nations such as China to allow themselves to borrow without limit – until the next crisis.

That leaves the Chinese yuan as the other serious challenger to the dollar. Its status today resembles that of the Japanese yen in the 1970s, when Japan was the world's second-largest economy and the biggest exporter but without an international currency. Like China, Japan had organised its growth period around financial repression – a series of rules to channel capital to domestic industry through government direction of credit, suppressed consumption and debt – and controls on foreign flows.

The change to floating currencies in the 1970s coincided with slowing growth and rising inflation. It led Tokyo to loosen credit and capital, just as today China is relaxing interest rates and welcoming foreign investment into its stock and bond markets. And like China today, in the 1970s Tokyo liberalised very slowly

and hesitantly, fearing exchange-rate volatility and competition from Western banks.

The US forced Japan to liberalise more quickly, which the country's central bankers welcomed to make the yen an international reserve currency. For a time in the 1980s the yen became important in forex markets and central bank reserves, but the central bank also allowed bank credit creation to shift from industry to real estate. This sparked the Japanese bubble, and its collapse in 1989 led to a decade or more of recession and retrenchment. The yen lost its relevance, even among Asian central banks, whose attention shifted to China and the financial hubs of Hong Kong and Singapore.

Despite its importance to global trade, China has likewise failed to make the yuan relevant to global payments or international bond issuance. It accounts for only about 2% of turnover in the global foreign-exchange markets, versus 88% for the dollar.

For several years, China has been opening the door to its stock and interbank bond markets – narrowly, usually via Hong Kong. It has also negotiated currency swaps with other central banks, so Chinese financial institutions can clear these trades directly without requiring them to go through the dollar. More recently, Beijing has been aggressively pursuing its Belt and Road Initiative, a project to connect Eurasia through Chinese-led infrastructure programmes.

On their own, these piecemeal initiatives will never enable the yuan to become a reserve currency, let alone displace the greenback. To do so would require the Communist Party to let go of important levers of control by building domestic financial markets that are deep, liquid and open to foreign capital.

China has been inventive, though. It has established an offshore yuan, a "hard currency" version that trades freely in Hong Kong and other places beyond mainland China. It enjoys a high valuation because there's strong international demand for mainland assets (China now has the world's third-largest bond market) but very little supply available to foreigners, at least for now. Meanwhile inside China, the government has been on a credit-creation binge. The tightly controlled funnel through the offshore yuan keeps the currency overvalued and masks its debasement at home.

Money is created in China as the government sets GDP growth targets and creates credit to meet that rate. During China's version of Les Trentes Glorieuses in 1979 to 2007, the rapidly growing economy needed all the money it could make. This policy is also part and parcel of the Communist Party's political system, which includes restrictions on information, a weak legal system and support for state-owned enterprises.

But in 2007, as growth slowed, China turned to credit creation to support the economy in the face of America's 2008 financial crisis. Growth has become dependent on debt, and the risk of a debt crisis is a good reason China is unlikely to pursue a "big bang" reform like the approach America took in the early 1900s to develop its capital markets or internationalise its currency.

That means for the yuan to take centre stage, the US dollar must first fall into a crisis of its own, sufficiently devaluing dollar-denominated assets so that China feels confident about opening its capital markets. This suggests a very different kind of transition than that of the guilder to sterling, or sterling to the dollar. This difference also calls to mind China's authoritarian political system. Holland, Britain and America were pluralist, democratic societies with checks and balances on central power. This separation is what gave people confidence in their currencies.

But history is not destiny; it is merely a guide. China has a reputation (perhaps overdone) for bureaucratic competence. Investors might crave stability over liquidity. The populist movements that emerged from the carnage of the global financial crisis are now roiling the West. That's one kind of instability. Another is coming from technology, particularly advances in artificial intelligence and big data. These are likely to wipe out white-collar jobs just as globalisation and financialisation gutted blue-collar workforces in developed countries.

China is at the forefront of these trends. Will its authoritarian government respond with a dystopian surveillance state, or will it come up with progressive solutions for the future of employment, wealth and stability? The experiences of its leading internet companies suggest some optimism is warranted. These companies have led the transition to electronic money. When it comes to attaining the world's primary reserve currency, China has more going for it than internationalising the yuan. It might reinvent money altogether.

PRIVATE CURRENCIES

Although national governments have monopolised what they consider legal tender, local communities have issued substitutes that have enjoyed success.

ITHACA HOURS: Since 1991, the town of Ithaca in New York has promoted its own currency called Ithaca hours, which is valid tender in many local shops (such substitutes for legal tender are called scrip). The purpose was to bring residents of the community together. Many cities now issue their own scrip, such as the Brixton pound (United Kingdom), the Salt Spring dollar (Canada) and the Fureai kippu (in Japan, for elderly communities).

CULION PESO: From 1901 till the 1950s, countries including Columbia, Japan, Malaysia and the US issued special notes and coins for use within leper colonies out of fear that lepers

might contaminate money and infect others (an idea that was debunked in 1938). The most prominent of these was a leper colony in Culion, in the Philippines, which issued aluminium coins from 1913 to 1930. Later, during the Japanese occupation, it issued emergency paper money for the lepers. The currency continued to be used into the 1980s, until leprosy became treatable and these colonies were shut down.

THE STELO: This global currency was invented in 1946 by the Universal League, an international society of enthusiasts of the Esperanto language. These utopians issued coins and coupons that they attempted to link to existing currencies, particularly the Dutch guilder. For a few years the stelo circulated among Esperantist societies, but efforts to maintain its stability to the guilder failed and by the 1960s it was effectively dead.

13
CRYPTO

The advent of cryptocurrencies means money is now stored as code on little pieces of hardware

The question of dollar dominance is not just about alternative currencies. It's also about the advent of cryptocurrencies, in which money is now based on mathematics and open-source code, rather than on faith in a government. China, the US and other countries are taking different paths, but there is no question that the world is on the cusp of monumental changes on par with the invention of coinage, paper money and commercial banking. We are about to redefine, once again, what we mean by "money" – what it is, who sets its rules and who benefits or suffers as a result.

The 1970s unleashed fiat money, the free movement of capital and the computerisation of financial markets. There is, however, a related history of electronic money. Initially this was a product of the dollar-based world. Today it might be a challenger.

An American 19th-century novelist, Edward Bellamy, predicted the credit card. His science-fiction book, "Looking Backward: 2000-1887", imagined the government distributing money as a public good via charge cards. He was wrong about the politics, but right about a system in which money became completely intangible, decoupled from physical coins or paper notes.

PLASTIC

The US created the first mass consumer market. By the early 1920s, Americans were beginning to borrow to take advantage of the boom in new goods, from radios to washing machines. But it was the automobile that had the biggest impact on consumer financing. Oil companies and hotel operators issued cards to travellers to make it easy for them to buy parts, fuel and lodging. These were "closed-loop" systems, however, in which the card's use was limited to the issuer's goods.

The first successful charge card launched in 1950 with Diners Club, which allowed business executives to eat at participating restaurants on credit. Diners Club then issued cards in plastic. For consumers this meant convenience, spending money they hadn't yet earned. Card issuers, meanwhile, were now creating money, like banks. Spending grows the economy, creating demand for goods and services, but it also creates debt and inflation. In the hands of card-issuing companies alone, the impact of plastic was modest. In 1958, however, Bank of America issued its own card, which could be used widely throughout the state of California. It invited smaller Californian banks to join its system, creating the network that became Visa.

Visa and Mastercard, which was formed by other banks in the 1960s, became massive payment systems connecting banks to merchants and consumers. These connections were then computerised.

Plastic was just one innovation that drove the consumer economy. In 1967, Barclays Bank installed the first automated teller machine at one of its London branches, creating a vending machine for cash. But cash machines took a long time to gain widespread acceptance, and although they are good at putting cash in depositors' hands, they do not create credit.

Charge cards, on the other hand, had a huge impact on consumer spending and spawned new forms of currency.

Once people had plastic cards in their pockets, it was a short step for companies to issue their own in the form of reward points. US airlines began issuing these to frequent fliers as early as 1972. Eventually these points could be traded for flights and then for other goods – transforming points into a proto-currency that could purchase real-world items.

Computer technology enabled credit and alternative currencies to expand at a vast scale. The same was true of electronic payments. Starting in the 1970s, the Federal Reserve began moving funds within its internal system electronically, eventually outpacing paper cheques. By 1975, the world's banking systems were linked electronically with the creation of the Society for Worldwide Interbank Financial Telecommunication (Swift).

In 2007, Safaricom launched M-Pesa, the first money transfer app based on mobile phones

This infrastructure paved the way for consumers to bank online as well as to make credit-card and inter-bank transactions electronic. In 1993, National Westminster Bank in the UK unveiled a plastic card called Mondex that doubled as a digital wallet. Consumers could store multiple currencies on it and use it to transfer money to other cardholders without having to go through the bank's systems (Mastercard subsequently bought the business).

But it wasn't until the advent of e-commerce in the 1990s that consumer banking moved online. Online commerce still accounts for only about 10% of US retail commerce. Most emerging markets remain almost entirely cash-based. Even now, about 1.7 billion people still lack a bank account, while credit cards remain accessible to just the wealthiest. But e-commerce is growing fast, and with it so are new forms of digital banking.

The Silicon Valley-based technology boom – transistors, semiconductors, the transfer of data into computer-readable ones and zeros – found early uses in financial services. Finance is about numbers and mathematics, which makes it an easy bedfellow for computerisation. In the 1970s, trading, payments and record-keeping began to be made electronic. The invention of the World Wide Web and browsers made the internet commercially useful, and companies like Amazon (founded in 1994) drove online commerce. In the 2000s this trend was turbocharged by the advent of Google's search engine, Facebook's social network and Apple's iPhone, whose introduction in 2007 popularised the smartphone.

Together these tech companies wrought profound changes in consumer behaviour, leaving banks behind. Banks were preoccupied with surviving financial crises and navigating loads of new regulation. Besides, their legacy systems and cultures were geared to interbank (wholesale) business, not customer service.

Into this gap stepped a new breed of Silicon Valley-inspired software companies, referred to as FinTechs, looking to get a piece of the financial pie, from payments to investments. Take PayPal as one example. The California-based technology company was founded in 1998 to develop security software for mobile devices. Then the company pivoted into money transfer services. It became the dominant payments processor to the rapidly growing world of online commerce. Within a decade the company was servicing more than 100 million user accounts across 25 different currencies.

PayPal was built for desktop computing. A new generation of FinTech is exploiting the smartphone. As commercial apps began to populate the iPhone, Apple partnered with American Express, Mastercard and Visa to launch Apple Pay. This debuted in 2013 and introduced digital tokens – a string of numbers – to replace the transfer of personal information, as a security measure. Computers had made money intangible and now tokenisation was separating money from a person's bank account.

But all of these innovations rely on existing banking and payments systems. PayPal and Apple Pay require your credit-card details to function.

Money was about to escape the gravity of the status quo.

E-MONEY
Technology is making it possible to extend financial services to people who have never had them. Mobile technology is creating a new wave of financial inclusion that will make digital money available to anyone on the planet who owns a smartphone – which is just about everybody.

Because technology is a global phenomenon, solutions that run on technology can be found anywhere, not just in California. In 2007, the Kenyan telecommunications operator Safaricom launched M-Pesa, the first money transfer application based on mobile phones (M stands for mobile and pesa is Swahili for money). People no longer needed a bank account to store money, transfer it or pay vendors. They could top up their M-Pesa accounts with cash deposited at one of many local mom-and-pop stores, just as they would to pay for airtime. Money became an SMS message.

M-Pesa is the first example of "electronic money" – debt-like instruments issued by a company, not a government, that are meant to be redeemable upon demand. E-money carries the full credit risk of the corporation behind it; there is no central bank or government to back it up if something goes wrong. But in places such as Kenya, where traditional banks ignored most people, the availability and convenience of e-money has made it wildly popular, giving tens of millions of people their first alternative to loan sharks when they need to borrow money.

Some governments have come to favour e-money, too, because it's easier to track for taxation purposes and physical cash is often used to fund illicit activities. In 2016, India's prime minister, Narendra Modi, demonetised most rupee banknotes in circulation. Although this led millions of people to open accounts with digital wallet providers, it also denied the economy the cash it required (for many poor people, demonetisation was simply government theft). There's no sign that demonetisation met Modi's goals. But India has also built a digital infrastructure of identity and payments, and with its vast population, it has emerged as a major battleground for e-money adoption and innovation.

To understand the impact of e-money on the banking sector, though, we must journey to China. Two of its companies, Alibaba and Tencent, have created vast financial empires that cut out banks almost entirely.

Jack Ma founded Alibaba in Hangzhou in 1999. His goal was to provide e-commerce within China and help small Chinese exporters sell to foreign customers.

By then, China had emerged as a manufacturing powerhouse based on the market reforms introduced by Deng Xiaoping, following the chaos of Mao Zedong's rule. But it remained financially backward.

The government owned all the banks, which were used to extend credit to state-owned enterprises and manage the expenses of government departments. Only in the 1980s did the government allow the first private consumer banks, followed by the opening of the Shanghai Stock Exchange in 1990, creating a heady but unreliable marketplace.

What Alibaba enabled in China was trust. Ordinary people believed transactions on Alibaba would be settled as promised. It became relevant to people in a way that the state-run financial sector never would. Alibaba launched AliPay in 2004 to expedite payments on its platform with zero transaction fees. It soon came to dominate payments in China, eclipsing the banks. Then it allowed account holders to invest unspent money in a money-market fund, which grew to be the world's largest. Alibaba has followed up with similar offerings in investments and insurance, catering to hundreds of millions of Chinese. All of this activity takes place on the company's servers, outside of any bank or third-party payment infrastructure.

Alibaba's biggest rival is Tencent, which launched in Shenzhen in 1998 as a messaging and gaming company but is now a vast conglomerate in entertainment, internet technology and artificial intelligence. It dominates social media in China with its WeChat messaging platform. WeChat became a super app, meaning it served as a portal to all kinds of services, including e-commerce, gaming, messaging and finance.

Tencent also developed payments. Its efforts took off in 2014 when the company created a means of digitally disbursing red packets for Chinese New Year. In Chinese culture, the red packet with its cash gift is a long-standing tradition. Now, by linking WeChat to a bank account, users could receive red-packet money from Tencent (through a contest) or transfer it to other WeChat users. In the month following this feature's debut, WeChat Pay's user base grew from 30m to 100m users and Tencent bit off a large chunk of AliPay's market.

Some governments are wary of crypto – China has gone so far as to ban its mining and trading

So now there are two giant closed-loop systems in China that between them provide to a billion people with financial services without reference to the banking system. They use the power of networks – for commerce and social media – to offer payments and other services that are fast, cheap and trusted. The timeless human activity of bilateral exchange is now being integrated into that of community, with money intertwined with personal photos and emojis. The marketplace hasn't been turbocharged in this fashion since ancient Greeks spent coins in the agora.

The rise of e-money in China is viewed as a triumph, but it also raises questions about how governments can protect consumers, protect privacy, manage systemic risks and – as Alibaba and Tencent extend their reach into other countries – cooperate with international authorities. It also pits e-money against bank money. Banks lose customers to internet companies, which costs them both deposits to fund their operations and the underlying data about those customers. At the same time, banks must pay high costs for branch networks, capital reserves and regulatory demands.

In poor countries like Kenya, banks have welcomed M-Pesa as a gateway service to bring people and companies into the formal financial system. But in China, banks are at risk of becoming completely dependent upon wholesale funding and limited to doing business with only large or state-owned companies. This might be a good thing for society if it makes banks compete harder to win customers. It's not so good for banks, which might become utilities, "dumb pipes" shuffling information on behalf of the internet companies that ate their lunch. Now these e-money models are being trialled in Hong Kong, in direct competition with global banks.

CRYPTOCURRENCIES
Computer scientists have been working on internet money or digital cash since the 1980s. What if computer programmers could invent new currencies that could be sent like email? What if the internet of information,

created by the World Wide Web, could become an internet of value?

The problem with digital cash was that computer files could be copied, and therefore the same money could be spent twice. You can't double-spend paper banknotes; once you hand them over, they're not yours anymore. But when you send a digital file, like an email or a photo, you're actually just copying it. In 2008, an anonymous computer programmer (or group of programmers) named Satoshi Nakamoto published a white paper that solved the problem of double-spending a digital file. He overcame this challenge by fusing digital cash with another idea also circulating in tech circles: blockchain.

A blockchain takes a ledger, just like the ones the Medicis used, and multiplies it across the marketplace. Bankers, be they from the house of Medici or the houses of JPMorgan and Citibank, keep their own books. These records might disagree and require intrusive paperwork to confirm and settle a transaction. Blockchain merges the ledgers into one so that all information shows up in everyone's books simultaneously and each transaction must be agreed on by the majority to be confirmed. Although the history of transactions is in the blockchain for all to see, they are all encrypted, so market participants can't tell which account belongs to whom.

Nakamoto called his protocol Bitcoin, and in early 2009 the first transaction was recorded, peer to peer, meaning there was no need for a bank or other intermediary such as Visa to process and settle the trade. Moreover, the transaction involved exchanging bitcoins, digital units of account that were to be "mined" by anyone with a computer service attached to the network, based on Nakamoto's software program. Bitcoins were created with two uses in mind: as a tool to facilitate payments anywhere in the world, any time, instantly, for free; and to serve as a store of value. The first cryptocurrency was born. Money was no longer a reflection of an issuer's power, but could be based on encoded mathematical formulae that distributes the minting and trading of money across an entire network of private computers.

The second cryptocurrency protocol, Ethereum, introduced smart contracts. This meant that money (in this case, ether) could be programmed. Computer code could replace the need for enforceable legal contracts to ensure money moved from place to place according to the arranged terms. No more lawyers – hooray!

Cryptocurrency now comes in a variety of forms: currencies, like bitcoin and ether; utility tokens, which are like reward points or debits meant to be redeemable for a service; securities tokens, which are forms of equity or debt in purely digital form; and stablecoins, which are meant to maintain their value relative to something else, like dollars or the price of gold.

An entire industry has emerged to enable crypto's mainstream adoption. Banks and corporations are also using aspects of blockchain technology to create more efficient ways to transact. They're doing this by driving industry-wide automation instead of relying on individual company processing.

Crypto is versatile, too. Just as Apple Pay introduced tokens to substitute for personal account information, crypto developers are working to tokenise assets. This could allow assets that were previously only tradeable in bulk to be parsed into tiny economic fractions. Digital coins could serve as tokens representing small, tradeable units of illiquid things such as commercial real estate and cargo ships, or intangible assets like patents or accessories in video games. Or they can be used to create derivatives of traditional securities so that people in poorer countries can access, say, Apple stock. All told, these assets could be transformed into money – trillions and trillions of dollars' worth – tradable on virtual exchanges.

For now, the crypto market is small and these nascent coins remain out of the hands of most people. They are still awkward to trade and store, and the infrastructure that has emerged, such as exchanges, has been repeatedly targeted by cybercriminals. The coins are also volatile, making them poor stores of value. Another problem with bitcoin is the huge drain on electricity required to mine blocks, making it environmentally dangerous.

Governments have been wary of crypto; China has gone so far as to ban its mining and trading. Others are trying to understand it so it can be regulated and taxed. Many authorities are concerned that bitcoin's anonymous and intangible nature has made it a tool for criminals and terrorists.

More fundamentally, governments can control banks. They can bring private credit creation to a halt by forcing banks to be fully reserved. But they can't control software released into the wild by bands of computer scientists who live all over the world.

THE FUTURE OF CURRENCY

Cryptocurrency's evangelists claim bitcoin will become the reserve currency of the future, replacing the US dollar as a new, electronic gold standard. They declare bitcoin to be a safe haven, particularly now that the world's major powers are flirting with a currency war, threatening the sort of beggar-thy-neighbour devaluations that haunted the 1930s and helped turn a recession into the Great Depression.

Bitcoin has endured for a decade, which is admirable, but its history is one of volatility, not stability. Perhaps over time it will evolve into a more reliable store of value. Today it is far too illiquid to serve as a safe haven for institutional investors. Might that change? Is bitcoin the new gold that will put an end to politicians' free-spending ways and the evils of money-printing by central banks?

Goldbugs, who call for the US government to return the dollar to the (real) gold standard, and bitcoin enthusiasts, who see software as the new "hard money", share an overlap of thought. These hard-money arguments fail because the explosion in credit their proponents disdain has been created by commercial banks, not by governments. People who think bitcoin is a viable standard are ignorant of the role of debt in financial history. Basing the money supply on gold or bitcoin would be deflationary and regressive, rewarding rich people and early technocratic adopters for holding otherwise useless assets instead of investing them in productive ventures. If the goal is to reduce inequality, then a global tax on capital or tougher reserve requirements on banks would be more effective.

But the world of digital finance is quickly expanding beyond cryptocurrencies, as the proliferation of utility tokens, securities tokens and stablecoins attests. Of these new forms of money, the potentially most revolutionary is a kind of stablecoin that allows new currencies to be invented on the back of pooled investments.

Facebook's proposed crypto coin is the most famous example of "investment money". Stablecoins originated as a safe place to park cryptocurrencies. If bitcoin was too volatile to trust holding onto, it could be swapped for a token whose value is pegged to, say, the US dollar.

Facebook has taken this concept a step further. With 2.7 billion users across its properties, Facebook has more users than any other internet company. But no Silicon Valley company has fused payments and financial services on top of its platform. This has so far been an Asian innovation, pioneered by WeChat and mimicked by Japanese and Korean peers.

But whereas WeChat has built a closed loop for its e-money, Facebook wants to create a currency that is built on blockchain. Such a cryptocurrency could become ubiquitous for payments, particularly in developing countries with lots of Facebook customers but still little in the way of financial services, digital or otherwise. With a nod to the Roman word for pound, Facebook wants to call its coin "Libra".

Libra is not a decentralised free-for-all like bitcoin. It is envisaged as a stablecoin that tracks a basket of leading fiat currencies like the dollar and the euro. Backers in Facebook's Libra consortium, which include a variety of big payment and technology companies but no banks, would invest money into a pool with a treasury function meant to manage the portfolio of underlying assets: fiat cash and short-term money instruments.

In some ways this represents an extension of the fiat world; Libra would be built on existing currencies. But it would become a currency unto itself that does not answer to the Fed or any other central bank. It would answer to backers, who would be basically equity shareholders in the fund behind Libra. It echoes the way Renaissance Italian bankers made IOUs tradeable, thus inventing the bond market. Facebook would create shares in its fund backing Libra, and both the coin and shares in the fund behind it would be tradable.

This has profound implications for how Libra could be used. Facebook's white paper imagines it as a catalyst for mass financial inclusion. In other words, it's a consumer product, just like other Facebook services. (Facebook is also setting up a company, Calibra, to offer financial services such as loans denominated in libra currency.) But Libra is also i-money, which means it can be traded and used by anyone, including banks, corporations and investment firms. Libra could easily become a new channel for vast capital flows or a unit of account for private credit creation.

In fact, because it's designed to be so convenient and easy to use, and because Facebook already has a global audience, it's likely Libra would become a global currency backing a gigantic, unregulated economy.

Connect this with the promise of cryptocurrencies to unlock trillions of dollars of value in currently illiquid assets (like real estate), and you have the makings of a tsunami of private money creation on a scale never seen before – and a true challenge to commercial banking and to a global financial system ordered around the US dollar.

Some aspects of Facebook's proposal should be welcomed. Innovation tends to extend access to vital financial services to people who are otherwise at the mercy of loan sharks or corrupt governments. As more business activities move onto digital ledgers (particularly blockchains), they become more transparent and accountable, notably to tax authorities. Commercial banks have gotten fat by charging consumers high fees for bad service, and Libra would represent welcome competition, especially once Facebook began extending loans and investment services using it.

However, Libra also threatens to bury what's left of the "great monetary settlement" – dating back to when another pound, the paper version of sterling, was introduced. The founding of the Bank of England, remember, was a compact between the government, which decided to bless private money creation, and bankers, who accepted regulatory oversight.

This unspoken but important accord allowed finance to support economic growth and the Industrial Revolution. Its renewal with the Bretton Woods system underlined rapid post-war recovery. It broke down in the 1970s. The fiat world has seen an unprecedented amount of unregulated money creation via futures, derivatives and shadow-banking activity related to securitisation. American and British regulators during the Great Moderation, preaching the gospel of laissez-faire economics, hammered in the final nail. The fruit of this was the 2008 global financial crisis.

Today, only 3% of the money in circulation is made by central banks: coins, paper notes, deposits held by commercial banks and foreign-exchange reserves. This includes the large sums created through quantitative easing by US, European and Japanese central banks. That means 97% of the money out there has been conjured by commercial banks and credit providers.

Now imagine what happens to that ratio when tokenisation of assets takes off and Facebook or other multinational corporations create blockchain-based currencies. And extrapolate that to today's world of the so-called elite one-percenters who own most assets versus everyone else, especially once artificial intelligence begins to scythe through white-collar employment. Public stewardship of financial markets would be swept away, and with it any accountability for the rich and the well-connected.

A different risk is that arrangements like Libra fail, creating a financial crisis of unimaginable destruction. Cyberattacks are one obvious hazard. But you don't need a hacker to create a run on the banking system. Stablecoins like Libra are built just like the monetary boards used to support currency pegs – the same kind of arrangements that were meant to keep sterling in line with the Deutsche mark, or the Swissie in line with the euro. Facebook's white paper referenced the Hong Kong dollar peg, but is this peg destined to last forever? History shows that such arrangements work until they don't.

This doesn't mean projects like Libra should be stopped or that bitcoin should be treated as a criminal conspiracy. Too many people around the world want to see digital finance succeed and classical finance has failed society in too many ways. Giving people access to new forms of payment and new opportunities to invest comes with tangible benefits. It's also possible that mass conversion by savers to e-money and i-money would reduce private-money creation because it would deny banks the deposits required to generate new loans. In other words, this scenario says digital finance would eventually replace fractional-reserve commercial banks.

A more likely outcome, at least for the medium term, is that both banks and digital finance endure, either as competitors or in new interlinked partnerships. Whether Libra specifically launches and succeeds may not matter: if it's not Libra, it will be something else.

So central banks, securities regulators and governments need to retool themselves to handle this new revolution in money and currency.

What is needed is a restitution of the "grand monetary settlement" fit for the 21st century. This must include new laws, greater international cooperation, and restructuring of central banks – both as regulators and as monetary stewards.

Some aspects of traditional regulation can be applied to digital finance: securities tokens, for example, are easy to fit into existing securities law. But finance based on blockchain is different because a token or

In some ways, today's emerging world of blockchain-based money marks a return to barter

cryptocurrency can represent both a company and a network. Laws governing financial markets are good at regulating companies; none were designed to manage networks involving computers connected from around the world.

International cooperation will be more important than ever. Governments will need to work with banks, technology companies and corporate issuers of tokens to develop a new set of standards for privacy, data, identity, reporting and taxation. In 2019, most countries, most notably the US, are ripping up the frameworks of international collaboration written in the 1940s. The world order has taken an unhappy turn. Risks of conflict are increasing. The 2008 financial crisis discredited the old financial world. We are experiencing a wrenching period of turmoil and change. Yet out of this will arise a new set of rules – for countries, for societies and for markets.

Governments should take a proactive and supportive view of digital money. Knee-jerk desires to clamp down are just as reckless as allowing a free-for-all. Those that recognise the need for a new monetary settlement have a better chance to determine what Nicholars Barbon's "imaginary value made by law for the conveniency of exchange" means today.

THE NEW MONETARY SETTLEMENT

Laws take a long time to pass and international cooperation is always hard. Easiest to adjust are domestic monetary policy and the roles of central banks.

During the Great Moderation, central banks were at the heart of finance, influencing markets by setting benchmarks for interest rates, adjusting the amount of capital commercial banks should reserve, and communicating preferences and intentions to the market. In return, central banks were given unprecedented leeway by politicians.

No more. The response to the GFC and the eurozone crisis was to use central bank balance sheets to buy assets from troubled banks, coupled with ultra-low interest rates – or even negative rates. This surely staved off a Great Depression. But central banks now find themselves unable to rid themselves of those assets on their books. Nor are they able to return interest rates to anything resembling "normal". When the next financial crisis or recession hits, no central bank will have the traditional tools at its disposal to stimulate credit. And politically it may not be possible for the Fed to act as the lender of last resort, especially if this is perceived as bailing out commercial lenders or taking another step towards hyperinflation.

Fiscal policy will play a greater role, as it did after the Second World War. Governments could pursue Keynesian strategies of reeling in spending during times of economic expansion and spending more on things like infrastructure projects to counter recessions. But we are still in the age of fiat money, and it is all too easy for politicians to simply borrow and spend more no matter the weather. However, industrial policy – the dirigisme of Les Trentes Glorieuses – is likely to make a comeback in Western countries, including the US.

Moreover, calls are growing for governments to issue as much money as they need to fully underwrite a basic salary for all citizens, on the assumption that computers will eliminate jobs en masse. This is sometimes bundled into an emerging argument called "modern monetary theory", or MMT.

MMT takes the view that money has always been the result of deliberate government attempts to direct the economy; so long as governments can raise taxes, they can pay for almost unlimited borrowing. Prudence be damned! This view ignores the history of private debt contracts that dates back to ancient Mesopotamia, the history of bills of exchange used by Muslim and Christian merchants to sidestep bans on usury and the fact that money today is mostly created by commercial banks.

MMT argues that fiat money has value because the government says so. This has been true of authorities that earned trust, such as the early Roman Empire,

the Amsterdam Exchange Bank, the Bank of England and the Federal Reserve. But plenty of governments squandered that trust, including the late Roman emperors, the Yuan and Ming emperors of China, the first American national banks and the Banque Générale. Indeed, John Law's belief that the Mississippi Company's shares had intrinsic value follows many of the same lines of reasoning as those behind MMT. And look how that turned out.

Fortunately, we have choices other than a bitcoin "hard currency" standard or unfettered, damn-the-consequences fiat. No government is going to abandon fiat money. Rather boringly, we must learn to manage fiat systems better. At the same time, we are going to complement fiat currency with a plethora of private digital money.

The best way to ensure this doesn't turn into a nightmare of a super-wealthy elite lording it over billions of disenfranchised people is to reassert a role for public oversight of digital finance. Relying on supervisory methods from the early 20th century won't suffice. One obvious remedy is for central banks to issue digital currencies. If you can't beat 'em, join 'em.

Central banks today are at the heart of finance because they safekeep the reserves of commercial banks. This lets central banks influence interest rates, but in return central banks also aid interbank payments, ensuring fairness among all national banks, large and small. What if this combination of obligations and service was extended to issuers of e-money or i-money?

Already, the People's Bank of China requires AliPay and WeChat Pay to deposit client funds as reserves, and other central banks are taking similar steps. Bringing e-money operators into the fold would provide them with a government backstop – thus removing the risk of a corporate bankruptcy – as well as enable them to transact with commercial banks on even terms.

In return, central banks enjoy a window into the creation and distribution of new e-money. By creating standards, they would require e-money wallets to be compatible and to meet the same requirements as commercial banks. (Today people can easily transfer money from their account to someone else's account at a different bank, but it's not yet possible to transfer money among closed-loop systems created by corporations.)

For this to work best, central banks will need to issue their own digital currency, which does not even require a blockchain. In 2017, Uruguay's central bank experimented with the first live e-peso, issuing 20m pesos' worth to 10,000 users via the local mobile phone company. The experiment continued for six months to test whether e-money would make taxes easier to collect. China is also likely to rely on mobile phones to transmit digital yuan. But there are many ways a government can issue digital cash.

The first risk of digital fiat currency is that central banks would have to take on a slew of new duties. They would now be regulating e-money and i-money operators, supervising everything from customer data management to system cyberattack defence. These worries can be mitigated, depending on how tech companies would access reserves and to what extent central banks could shift the onus of regulation and security to private companies.

The second risk is that, taken to its logical conclusion, e-money users – you and me – might need to be granted our own central bank accounts. After all, if a central bank issues digital fiat, a mirror of its paper notes in blockchain form, then individuals and small businesses could also operate that money.

China has indicated it will restrict digital yuan to the interbank market. This would make the wholesale payments system more efficient but limit the currency's circulation. Uruguay issued its e-pesos directly to individuals but limited its experiment and didn't allow people to hold reserves directly at its central bank. This meant the money could be used anonymously.

For some central banks, increasing oversight of the currency might be important. But universal access to digital cash would set the central bank in direct competition with commercial banks. That could be dangerous. Imagine if there were a crisis like the one involving Lehman Brothers. Would depositors keep their money with a commercial bank when they could entrust their savings to the central bank instead? The reasonable answer is no. Commercial banks would see their deposits rush for the exit, turning a crisis into an all-out collapse.

The same risk goes for authorities in emerging markets. In a pinch, would depositors stick with local-currency holdings or switch everything into, say, Libra coins or the digital fiat of a big neighbour such as China or the EU?

Those are the risks. But there are also opportunities. Digital currency would enable central banks to directly manipulate interest rates instead of setting benchmarks for commercial lenders to follow. They can even go one step further, paying a yield on digital cash to encourage its uptake (or charge people to hold their currency, an option that might appeal to the Swiss National Bank).

Getting more people and businesses to use digital cash would also give the central bank far greater, instant visibility into money creation and flows, helping it make better decisions. Remember the boring call for better market governance? Well, monitoring the market in real time via digital fiat currency might to make that possible. Digital money is also traceable, which appeals to the tax authorities and police, but which obviously calls for rules about how anonymous this new cash could be. Further, digital fiat would pose a threat to private cryptocurrencies such as bitcoin because it would be more liquid and better suited as collateral and could bear a yield.

Most of all, central banks would be able to set standards and influence the rules of the game. Among these must be guidelines to avoid "too big to fail" situations. Blockchain requires networks, and network effects tend to concentrate gains, leading to monopoly. Central banks should ensure monopolies behave as public utilities and don't enjoy outsized rewards for simply existing. A third rule central banks should lay out is a playbook in the event of a crisis, such as a stablecoin default, in order to minimise disruptions to the financial system.

Central bank digital currencies are close to becoming a reality: in August 2019, the People's Bank of China (PBoC) indicated that its plans for a digital yuan were ready to be implemented. The PBoC has been studying this since 2014 and has gained a sophisticated understanding of the economics. This will surely convince other monetary authorities to follow suit, and many will view the PBoC's digital yuan as the model.

But not every form of digital fiat will be the same. Depending on local culture and conditions, some central banks might want to extend reserves to all citizens in return for a greater role in guiding markets and supervising activity. Others might keep reserves at a wholesale level for large companies and keep the onus on compliance, systems and security on them. They will come up with different rules for market integrity, privacy and underlying market infrastructure.

This has implications for the future of the dollar as the world's paramount reserve currency. One use case for a digital yuan could be for China to apply it externally in its Belt and Road Initiative, financing infrastructure projects across Eurasia via an electronic ledger operated out of Beijing. This could be a way for China to challenge the US dollar by making digital yuan an important reserve currency, without the Communist Party having to undergo painful domestic reforms of its economy.

Will China seek a new version of the "great monetary settlement"? The country is run by a Leninist party that insists on controlling the commanding heights of the economy. What goes for the analogue world will surely apply to one built on ones and zeros. If China becomes the first, and perhaps the most important, issuer of central bank digital currencies, does it get to set the rules for 21st-century finance?

Looking to history, we know trust in money cannot be declared or imposed from above without creating a crisis. Trust must be earned. That's true for Facebook and the Chinese government alike.

As for ordinary people, these changes are already affecting our lives. For many people in wealthy cities, coins and paper have already disappeared. Sweden is now almost entirely cashless. Soon, only the poorest will think of money as physical objects filling our pockets.

This trend has been about replacing cash with credit cards, meaning it's still bound to the commercial banking system. But digital finance enables value to be exchanged via the internet, such as through an email or a WhatsApp message. Just as coins and then paper money influenced the way people thought and calculated, the internet of value will give us new perspectives on exchange. Money is becoming more social, more personalised. It is being associated more with goals (let me help you buy a house) than financial processes (let me sell you a mortgage).

In some ways we are returning to the distant past, the mythical time of barter, with commodities brokers replaced by peer-to-peer networks enabling us to buy and sell what we want via an electronic platform. Some of these are simple, centralised networks such as crowdfunding sites like Kickstarter. But squint your eyes, and look at more disruptive technologies such as blockchain. These could disrupt even Amazon and Alibaba by decentralising the matching engines for goods, just as bitcoin has done for money.

Maybe we won't even think of money as how much is in our account anymore. Rather we will regard each other in the language of credit, with algorithms instead of bankers or assessors telling us how much we can trust someone to deliver a service or pay back a loan. The entire economy is digitising, transforming our everyday behaviour into data that can be measured and monetised by machines.

Money has always been a metaphor, standing for something else. Perhaps within our lifetime, it will come to stand for us.

SCI-FI MONEY

Movies and science-fiction novels can be prescient about the future of money. In 1887, novelist **EDWARD BELLAMY** predicted the credit card. More recently, **CORY DOCTOROW** ("Down and Out in the Magic Kingdom") describes a world in which computer chips in our brains connect us to an all-encompassing peer-to-peer network.

NEAL STEPHENSON'S "Cryptonomicon" predicted the token-isation of gold, and **IAIN BANKS'S** "Consider Phlebas" described coins that convert into chemical elements. Currency in the Harry Potter books by **JK ROWLING** is created with time limits – something smart contracts on Ethereum could do today.

Some works of sci-fi imagine currencies with retro Roman-sounding names. in **FRANK HERBERT'S** "Dune", the commodity-money spice powers the economy, supported by a currency called the solari. In the "Star Trek" universe, the mercantile Ferengi use a coin called latinum that can't be counterfeited – perhaps Satoshi Nakamoto is actually one of them? And in "Battlestar Galactica", the unit is the cubit.

In both "Star Trek" and "Star Wars", and in many other sci-fi books and movies, money is simply referred to as credits. This may seem bland but is perhaps closer to what money may become.

But given the somewhat absurd nature of money, it might be worth concluding with a quote from **DOUGLAS ADAMS'** "The Hitchhiker's Guide to the Galaxy":

> *In fact there are three freely convertible currencies in the Galaxy, but none of them count. The Altairian Dollar has recently collapsed, the Flainian Pobble Bead is only exchangeable for other Flainian Pobble Beads, and the Triganic Pu has its own very special problems. Its exchange rate of eight Ningis to one Pu is simple enough, but since a Ningi is a triangular rubber coin six thousand eight hundred miles along each side, no one has ever collected enough to own one Pu.*

The Yap islanders, with their giant stone discs, come to mind. Yet it worked. Space age or stone age, people have always invented rules to keep score.

WORKS CONSULTED

BOOKS

Adshead, SAM, "Tang China: The Rise of the East in World History", Palgrave Macmillan, 2004

Brands, HW, "The Money Men: Capitalism, Democracy, and the Hundred Years' War Over the US dollar", Atlas Books, 2006

Davies, Glyn, "A History of Money: From Ancient Times to the Present Day", third edition, University of Wales Press, 2002

Dillon, Patrick, "The Last Revolution: 1688 and the Creation of the Modern World", Pimlico, 2007

Eagleton, Catherine and Williams, Jonathan, "Money: A History", British Museum Press, second edition, 2007

Eichengreen, Barry; Mehl, Arnaud; and Chitu, Livia, "How Global Currencies Work: Past, Present and Future", Princeton University Press, 2018

Ferguson, Niall, "The Ascent of Money: A Financial History of the World", Penguin Press, 2008

Gordon, Peter, and Morales, Juan Jose, "The Silver Way: China, Spanish America and the Birth of Globalisation, 1565-1815", Penguin Books, 2017

Gordon, Stewart, "When Asia Was the World", Da Capo Press, 2008

Kay, John, "Other People's Money", Profile Books, 2015

Kindelberger, Charles, "Manias, Panics, and Crashes: A History of Financial Crises", third edition, John Wiley & Sons, 1996

Sehgal, Kabir, "Coined: The Rich Life of Money and How Its History Has Shaped Us", Grand Central Publishing, 2015

Mann, Charles, "1493: How Europe's Discovery of the Americas Revolutionized Trade, Ecology and Life on Earth", Granta, 2011

Phillips, Kevin, "Wealth and Democracy: A Political History of the American Rich", Broadway Books, 2002

Picketty, Thomas, "Capital in the Twenty-First Century", translated by Arthur Goldhammer, Belknap Press, 2014

Turner, Adair, "Between Debt and the Devil: Money, Credit, and Fixing Global Finance", Princeton University Press, 2016

Weatherford, Jack, "The History of Money: From Sandstone to Cyberspace", Three Rivers Press, 1997

ANCIENT WRITERS

Herodotus, "The Histories", paragraph 94, via Ancient History Encyclopedia, www.ancient.eu

Ibn Battuta, "Travels in Asia and Africa: 1325-1354", translated by H.A.R. Gibb, 1925

Kautilya, "Arthashastra", 8: 3.30-3.35

Polo, Marco, "The Travels of Marco Polo", part one, chapter XXVI, translated by Henry Young

VIDEOS

Martin, Felix, "What is Money, and Why Does it Matter?", speech at St Paul's Institute, YouTube video, February 5th 2014

Parker, Ed and Professor Parker, Geoffrey, "History of Derivatives: Ancient Mesopotamia to Trading Places", YouTube video, December 17th 2014

Vague, Richard, "The Debt We Don't Talk About", YouTube video, March 28th 2018

Werner, Richard, "Today's Source of Money Creation", YouTube video recorded at The Money Institute, February 5th 2018

Yong, Stanley, "Desirability & Necessity of a CBDC for Blockchains", YouTube video, July 10th 2018

JOURNALS, MANUSCRIPTS & WEBSITES

Adrian, Tobias, and Mancini-Griffoli, Tommaso, "The Rise of Digital Money", Fintech Notes, International Monetary Fund, July 2019

British Museum, www.britishmuseum.org/explore/themes/money

DiBiasio, Jame, "CLSA's Cochran: central banks likely to issue crypto", www.DigFinGroup.com, December 12th 2018

French, Howard, "Africa's Lost Kingdoms", The New York Review of Books, June 27th 2019

Ghazanfar, Shaikh, "Capitalist Traditions in Early Arab-Islamic Civilization", part 3, www.muslimheritage.com

Hobson, John, "Islam's Historical Contribution to Commerce and Finance", www.muslimheritage.com

International Swaps and Derivatives Association factsheet, www.isda.org

Jasperse, Jitske, "Manly Minds in Female Bodies: Three Women and Their Power Through Coins and Seals", Humboltd University of Berlin, October 2018

Kaplan, Edward, "Chinese Economic History from Stone Age to Mao's Age", manuscript version 2.2, chapter 7, 1997, Western Washington University

Licandro, Gerardo, "Uruguyan e-peso on the context of financial inclusion", Banco Central del Uruguay presentation to Bank of International Settlements, November 16th 2018

Munchau, Wolfgang, "The unbreakable, unsustainable eurozone", Financial Times, April 29th 2019

Quinn, Stephen and Roberds, William, "The Big Problem of Large Bills: The Bank of Amsterdam and the Origins of Central Banking", 2005, www.repec.org/sed2005/up.12983.1106676974.pdf

Taylor, Bryan, "The Rise and Fall of the Largest Corporation in History", Business Insider, November 6th 2013

West, Mark, "Private Ordering at the World's First Futures Exchange", Michigan Law Review, vol. 98, no. 8, August 2000

World History Biz, "Mesopotamian Money and Weights", www.worldhistorybiz.com, May 9th 2015

Wikipedia entries including "Fugger", "History of Chinese currency", "Price Revolution".

ABOUT JAME DIBIASIO

Jame DiBiasio is an award-winning financial journalist based in Hong Kong. He is currently founder and editor of DigFin Group, a website covering digital finance, at www.digfingroup.com. He is a published author of thrillers and history. Follow him on LinkedIn or visit him at www.jamebooks.com.

ABOUT HARRY HARRISON

Based in Hong Kong, Harry Harrison is a freelance cartoonist perhaps best known for his daily political satire in the *South China Morning Post*. However, his work has also appeared internationally in publications such as *IFR, The Guardian, Time Magazine, The Wall Street Journal Asia* and the *Far Eastern Economic Review*, occasionally picking up awards along the way. He is a proud member of the UK's Professional Cartoonists' Organisation. www.procartoonists.org/portfolios/harryharrison.

ABOUT OANDA

In 1996, OANDA became the first organisation to share exchange rate data free of charge on the internet, launching an FX trading platform that helped pioneer the development of internet-based currency trading five years later. Today, OANDA provides online multi-asset trading, payments, money transfers and currency data to corporates and consumers alike, demonstrating an unrivalled expertise in foreign exchange. Regulated by seven major authorities and with offices in the world's most active financial markets, the firm remains dedicated to transforming the business of foreign exchange. For more information, please visit oanda.com.

Lightning Source UK Ltd.
Milton Keynes UK
UKHW020759101120
373087UK00002B/175